MANILA MEMORIES

Four Boys Remember Their Lives
Before, During and After the Japanese Occupation

*To Len Andrew who spent
years of his life in asia.*

Juergen R. Goldhagen

10/14/20

MANILA MEMORIES

Four Boys Remember Their Lives
Before, During and After the Japanese Occupation

Hans Hoeflein

Roderick Hall

Juergen R. Goldhagen

Hans Walser

edited by
Juergen R. Goldhagen

Published in the United Kingdom in 2008 for Old Guard Press
by Shearsman Books Ltd
58 Velwell Road
Exeter EX4 4LD
to whom permissions enquiries should be directed.

ISBN 978-1-84861-010-1

Book design by Birgit Schroeter

TABLE OF CONTENTS

DEDICATED TO OUR PARENTS
WHO BROUGHT US THROUGH IT

コレヒドール島

（陸軍派遣畫家）　猪熊弦一郎氏筆

A postcard depicting a Japanese soldier.

PREFACE

In addition to myself, the other storytellers are Roderick Hall, Hans Hoeflein and Hans Walser. We are close in age, and were all students at the American School on Donada Street in Pasay, before and after the war, but I got to know them well in High School after the war ended. These stories are mainly about our lives between the years of nine and twelve, as we remember them, some sixty-five years later. Using written and oral interviews, I have combined all of our experiences into this book. The chapters are in chronological order, and our stories are set down separately in each time frame.

A few of us in my graduating class of 1950 at the American School of Manila, generally Swiss, Germans and Italians, were considered by the Japanese to be neutrals, or allies. While the Japanese in Manila considered us friendly allies, Hans Hoeflein and I would have been treated differently back in Germany. I hope that our stories, briefly told, will give future historians insights into life in Manila before the war, during the war, and after the war, from the viewpoint of four youths.

The idea for this book grew out of a seminar on war experiences held at an American School of Manila reunion for the Classes of 1945-55. Fellow alumni and authors Mary McKay Maynard, of *My Faraway Home* and Doreen Gandy Wiley, of *One Hundred Candles* encouraged us all to put down our memories. Here are ours.

I want to especially thank those who helped me edit the book, including Prof. Ricardo Trota Jose and my wife, Sue Ford-Goldhagen. Thanks also to Birgit Schroeter and Rod Hall for helping with layout and design.

Juergen R. Goldhagen
Fearrington Village, North Carolina
June, 2008

Many books have been written about experiences in Manila and the Philippines during World War II by soldiers, guerrillas, prisoners in Santo Tomas and those who hid in the countryside. A few books describe the experiences of foreigners caught in Manila by the war. To my knowledge, none were written from the perspective of young European boys who, for a variety of reasons, spent the occupation years in Manila, but were not interned.

PART 1

LIFE BEFORE THE WAR

CHAPTER I

BEGINNINGS

JUERGEN GOLDHAGEN'S NARRATIVE

At about 8:30 p.m. on January 15, 1931, I was born in an apartment in Hannover, Germany, with the help of a midwife. My parents were Charlotte and Martin Goldhagen, and I was baptized Juergen Richard Max Goldhagen.

My earliest memories are of living in a room near some elevated train tracks and saying, "Baboof, baboof," in imitation of the engines. I also remember a high window that I had fallen out of while Dad was looking after me. Luckily, I landed on a roof just beneath the window. Otherwise, it would have all ended right then—we lived on the second or third floor of the building.

Dad originally came from Duisburg, where he was orphaned at about age eight. He was raised by a rich uncle—Dad was never supposed to have to go to work. Unfortunately, his uncle lost his money during the German inflation of the 1920s by investing in German government bonds.

Dad worked for the Allgemeine Elektrizitaetsgesellschaft A.G. from 1919 to 1933. That year, he lost his job and then could not get another one because he was Jewish.

Having been in the German army during the First World War, he saw all the military preparations going on and decided

Map of Germany

that there was another war coming. This, coupled with his not being able to get a job, made him decide to leave Germany. Friends of his had gone to the Philippines, and wrote that it was a good place to live and that they could get him a job, so, Dad went to Manila in 1935.

We didn't have enough money to pay for all of us to go, so, Mom and I stayed in Hannover until 1937, when Dad had made enough money to send for us. Mom was a master tailoress, and she supported us by making and repairing clothes and suits for her rich clientele. In those days, a lot of clothing was still handmade and not bought off the rack. Thanks to her expertise, we never starved.

I didn't miss Dad because after he left, Mom and I moved into the same apartment building where my cousin Wolfgang lived, and he and I became like brothers. Before Dad left, whenever we visited Wolfgang, I always played with his huge box of toys, and now I could play with him and the toys all the time. Wolfgang's father—my Uncle Harry—was a big, handsome man in an SA stormtrooper uniform and I used to love it when he would carry me on his shoulders. Even better, my grandmother, Oma Dora, also lived in the same apartment as Wolfgang, so I had more than enough family to replace my father. Besides, Mom was with me.

Juergen Goldhagen – 1941

Life was really good to me. I played with my cousins, Wolfgang and Lore, as well as with lots of other kids on the street. Some memories include being nearly run over by a car that squealed to a halt as I chased a ball into the street; throwing a ball onto another cousin's birthday cake; giving the Nazi salute to a parade of marching soldiers; going to a nearby park to play in the sandlot and envying some kids with neat military toys; and just having lots of fun.

One thing that was not fun was my seeing observer balloons. For some reason, I was terrified of them. Once, while visiting my cousin Lore in the suburbs, I saw some on the horizon, and I screamed and pounded on the front door to be let in to hide from them. Eventually, I got over my fear and one day in Hannover, one with a big Swastika on it flew low overhead and I stood and watched while my friends ran away in fear.

We also had air-raid drills and one time we had to go into the basement of the building where we were living, No. 17 Birkenstrasse. This proved to be prophetic because the building was later destroyed in one of the bombing raids.

One day, Mom got a call telling her to report to Gestapo headquarters. She was really terrified. But all they did was tell her that they knew that she was married to a Jew who lived in the Philippines, and that they would never let her leave Germany because she had a son and the Reich needed all the males it could get.

In 1937, my cousin Wolfgang started going to school and I was a little jealous. Because I was too frail for my age, being skinny and underweight, the school would not accept me until I had gotten a bit hardier. Mom didn't care because we were going to be leaving anyway.

One day, I came home from playing on the street and I asked Mom if I had two names. Mom said, "No, why do you ask?" I replied, "Because all the kids are calling me Jude," even though I had been baptized a Lutheran, my mother's faith. At that point, Mom decided it was time to leave. Fortunately, by then Dad had saved enough money to send for us. So, we said good-bye to all our friends. I remember visiting a friend of my mother's and carrying a little black suitcase that had been filled with candy wrapped in strips of colored cellophane. I was very fond of that suitcase and kept it for years after we reached Manila.

In November 1937, we took the train to Hamburg to board the *Gaasterkerk*, a Dutch freighter. At the train station, I had managed to get separated from Mom, and Uncle Harry found me just in time to hand me to Mom through a window as the train pulled out. Some of our relatives went with us and stayed in Hamburg overnight as we did not sail until 8:00 the following morning.

Juergen and his mom on the way to Manila in 1937.

According to Mom, a bureaucrat who was a good friend of the family had made sure that we were able to get the necessary papers to leave and had come along to make sure there would be no last-minute hitch.

Even when we were on the ship, Mom was afraid the Gestapo would come aboard and take us off. The ship's captain assured her that the Gestapo would not be allowed to take us off a Dutch ship, but (as we now know) if they had wanted to do so, they would have.

A postcard showing the ship *Gaasterkerk* (Holland)

Even the American Consul in Hamburg gave Mom a tough time. For some reason, he did not want to give us a permanent visa to the Philippines. Recently, after viewing a TV show on this subject, I realized it must have been because the American Diplomatic Corps was trying to prevent Jews from entering the US and its territories. Mom was able to get a visitor's visa, and once we arrived in the Philippines we did not leave until years after the war.

When the ship's whistle blew, Mom and I both jumped because it was so loud. This was the start of a long and lonely voyage for me. Although there were several couples on board, there were no other kids. We went through the Suez Canal and the entire trip took about six weeks. As we passed through the canal, a British warship preceded us and I was impressed by its size. In Aden, a magician came aboard and, when he pulled an egg out of my ear, I was terribly frightened and started crying. In Colombo, Ceylon, we went ashore and I became temporarily separated from my Mom and the captain in a place with a row of wide columns. So, they hid behind one and when I turned around they were gone. Needless to say, I was really scared and they had the last laugh on me.

When we sailed into the tropics, they set up a swimming pool on deck and we went swimming. Although I was wearing some type of flotation device, I clung for dear life to Mom because no one had told me that the life preserver wouldn't keep me upright. I kept tipping to the side and was convinced that the thing was not going to keep me afloat.

RODERICK HALL'S NARRATIVE

Unlike Juergen and Hans Hoeflein, I was born in the Philippines on November 7, 1932, in the Hospital Español de Santiago in Makati, Rizal. Then on the outskirts of Manila, Makati is now the banking, commercial, and executive residential center of Metro Manila.

I was the first child of Alaistair Cameron Hall, from Edinburgh, Scotland, and Consuelo McMicking, who was born in Manila. There were soon four of us: Ian, born in 1934, Alaistair in 1936, and Consuelo in 1937.

My mother's Spanish-Scottish family was part of the old Spanish upper class. Her father's Scottish family had been trading in the Philippines, originally in Iloilo, since the early 1800s. I was told that a McMicking had been the Captain of the first iron-hulled vessel to enter Manila Bay. The family trading company, founded about 1815 as McMicking & Ker, I believe is still in business today as Ker & Co. Grandfather, who was born in Iloilo, had started his career as a lawyer, and served as the High Sheriff of Manila from about 1900 to 1918. In his capacity as the senior legal officer of the city, grandfather was the plaintiff in numerous cases before the Philippine Supreme Court and, in at least one instance, the US Supreme Court. In 1918 he became the Senior Manager of The Insular Life Assurance Company, the oldest life insurance company in the Philippines, founded in 1910. My maternal grandmother, Angelina Rico, was born in Manila.

Hans Hoeflein on the Island of Ibiza (Spain) in 1935 (age 4).

My father, Alaistair Cameron Hall, 6'4" tall and known to all his friends as "Shorty" Hall, arrived in Manila in 1924 at the age of twenty-one, with Smith Bell & Co., an English trading company. He learned to speak fluent Spanish, but always kept his Scottish burr. My parents met in Manila, and were married in June, 1930. In 1933 Dad left Smith Bell & Co. to establish Ovejero & Hall, a firm trading in stocks, bonds and commodities. By the start of the war it had become one of the leading stockbrokers in Manila.

HANS HOEFLEIN'S NARRATIVE

I was born in Cologne, Germany, on July 17, 1931. My father was Justin Hoeflein and my mother was Margaret Hoeflein. In Germany, the name was spelled Hoflein with an umlaut, or with two small dots over the "o". When they got to Manila, my parents changed the name to Hoeflein because the typewriters didn't have an umlaut symbol.

In 1933, when I was about one and a half years old, my Dad received a telephone call tipping him off that he was about to be arrested on trumped-up charges that he had murdered two Nazi officials. I don't know who the caller was, but I think it may have been from the company my Dad worked for, Klöckner-Humboldt-Deutz, because Dad was highly thought of and the company wanted to protect him. At 30 years of age, he was already the export manager of that multinational company, and such rapid promotion was most unusual and a reflection of his abilities. He was also the chairman of the Socialist Party in Cologne and that party was very anti-Nazi, which is why I think the Nazis trumped up the charges.

We immediately took a train to Madrid, Spain, leaving all our possessions behind. Since we had been renting an apartment, I don't think we left that much behind, or friends may even have forwarded our stuff to us. On my fifth birthday, we were on

The cargo-passenger liner *Gneisenau*, built in 1935 could carry 186 First Class and 150 Tourist Class passengers. She was sunk by a mine in the Baltic Sea, en route to Russia with German troops, on May 21, 1943.

vacation in the Mediterranean when the Spanish Civil War started. The German embassy then evacuated all Germans, and Mom and I went by train to Barcelona and then by ship back to Germany. From there we went to Portugal and were reunited with Dad. We lived in Cascais, a fishing village near Lisbon.

In 1937, Dad's company told him that war was coming and that they were going to send him as far from Europe as possible. So, we ended up going to the Philippines. We sailed from Genoa, Italy, on the SS *Gneisenau*, a German ship via Port Said; Colombo, Ceylon; and Singapore. We arrived in Manila on August 10, 1937, after about a three-week trip.

The Manila News Bulletin of August 11, 1937 listed new passenger arrivals.

Passenger Arrivals

Per s. s. *Gneisenau* from Bremen, Southampton, Genoa, Port Said, and Singapore:—Ailene Herbst, Karl Koesting, Emily Harridge, Dolores Gregory, Arthur Neville, Frederick Hagedorn, Esperanza Hagedorn, Jose Yulo and family, Gregoria Concepcion, Maria Macafe, Teodora Dejas, Pablo ria Macafe, Teodora Dejas, Pablo Edwin Ronan, August mma Leukart, Carlos Montilla, Salvador Benedicto, Dr. Howe, Ravael Alunan, Alunan, Hermenigildo and family, Wilhelmus Shimoto, Samuel Leitne Bannink, Olaf Kasner and family, Hubert Ghysens, Armand Lamineur, Jose Inzy-Barica, August Auer, Elsa Auer, Justin Hoeflein and family, Celso Sandoval, Gregorio Villaserau, K. Gantner, F. Kreill, C. Blanco and Osamu Fujita.

Per s. s. *Pres. Jefferson* from

's s. *Pres. Jefferson* trom ttle, Japan and China: Ang Tiao, Mrs. Frank G. Ashbrook, E. Baker, M. Balawit, C. W. man, W. F. Blake, Mrs. L. danoff, Miss Eunice Bowman, s Helen Boyle, Miss H. Bryans, E. M. Burns, Miss M. Car-

Aug. 29
Aug. 30
Aug. 31
MOON:—New moon, Aug. 6; quarter, Aug. 29, 1937.—Da

BURNS. P

HANS WALSER'S NARRATIVE

I was born at the Hospital Español (the same hospital as Rod), Makati, Rizal, a suburb of Manila, Philippine Islands, on March 23, 1933. My parents were Jean Walser and Ruth McCracken Walser.

Jean Walser was born February 20, 1897 in Herisau, Switzerland, the first of 2 boys. His birth name was Johann Jakob Walser. After high school he went to a business school in Soleure, the French speaking section of Switzerland, where he had his name legally changed to Jean, the French equivalent of Johann. He went to the Philippines, arriving in Manila in July 1920. He went to work for Menzi Inc., a British firm in the import/export business, starting at their branch in Iloilo, Philippines. Two years later he transferred to their office in Manila. My father, being the typical Swiss, spoke several languages fluently, but my mother, being American, spoke only one; so English was the only language spoken at home. It was always interesting listening to two Swiss talking to each other as they would start off in one language, run into a word that was better expressed in another language, switch to that language and continue on in that language till the next change came. And the Swiss in Manila had to speak Spanish and generally knew a smattering of Tagalog and Cantonese.

My mother was born February 20, 1900 in Mechanicsville, Iowa, the middle child of 1 boy and 2 girls of Clarence McCracken and Emily Thomas McCracken. (My mother and father had the same birthday, February 20th, and by fate (?) my wife and I have the same birthday, March 23rd.) Clarence was the eleventh child of twelve, the first 7 having died before their twelfth birthday. He graduated from Indiana Normal in 1894 with a Bachelor of Science degree and went on to become a superintendent of schools in Iowa. My mother went to high school in Des Moines, Iowa, graduating in 1917 and then attended Drake University. After 2 years at Drake she became a high school teacher in mathematics. I do not know why she left Drake after 2 years. After 2 years teaching high school, she quit and returned to college, going to the University of Chicago in Illinois, the best math school in the country at that time. There she graduated and was awarded a scholarship for excellence in mathematics. She then continued her education in mathematics at the University of Chicago and attained her Master's degree March 18th, 1924, a rare thing for a woman in that day. The vice president of the Philippines was in the United States at that time and looking for teachers for the University of the Philippines. It is hard to imagine, but this single young mid-western Iowan woman, in 1924, took a month long trip by herself on a steamer to Manila to teach mathematics at the University of the Philippines. I wonder what her parents thought at the time.

My mother and father met in Manila and were married March 13, 1926 at the Union Church, the only Protestant church in Manila. I was born 7 years later. At the age of 4, I was enrolled in kindergarten at the American School and continued in that school until the war broke out. (All 4 of the writers of this story eventually graduated from high school at the American School).

CHAPTER II

LIFE BEFORE THE WAR

JUERGEN GOLDHAGEN'S NARRATIVE

At dawn on December 8, 1937, we arrived in Manila Bay. I would have been even more excited had I known what was going to happen on that date four years later.

When the boat docked, a host of brown men came aboard. Who were all these brown men? No one had told me that the Filipinos were brown, and I was totally surprised and bewildered. Then, Mom pointed out a fat white man and said that was my father. My reaction was not one of joy. Dad was bald, fat and not good looking. Not at all like my tall, dark and handsome storm trooper, Uncle Harry.

The first place where we lived was a boarding house off Harrison Boulevard in Pasay. It was run by Lottie Schoenert, a German lady, and once again there were no kids except for me. She did have books though, and I remember looking at some German books about the First World War that had colored pictures of German planes on a night raid. There were also some books with steamship pictures in them and I would try to draw the ships. She used to cook a delicious German dish called Milchreis (milk rice). The rice is boiled until it is very soft, and is served with lots of milk and cinnamon topping. My first experience with rice.

At that time, my folks gave me a toy tin battleship that had been made in Japan and I didn't like it because it was not as solid as my German toys. Later, when the real Japanese battleships came, they were solid enough. I started to learn English at a Jewish school and then went to the Philippine Normal School, which was a public school. I was very unhappy there because I was the only white kid in my class. A few of the Filipino kids were friendly, but some wanted to fight me because I was white. I didn't want to fight anyone. I just wanted to be with friends.

At that time, I was so lonely that I wished I had black hair and brown skin like a Filipino, instead of being blonde and white. Once, I wrapped a thread around my finger and the tip became purple from the poor circulation. The color was more like the Filipinos, so why couldn't the rest of me be that color? No, I did not try to wrap the rest of my body in thread. There was a Spanish boy my Mom would take me to and we would try to play, but he didn't speak German and I couldn't speak English. All I wanted to do was go back to Germany.

In 1938, we moved to Aldecoa Street, still living with Lotte Schoenert. She had a loyal string of boarders who moved with her because she was an excellent cook and kept an efficient boarding house. Once, I got into her jewelry box and played with it for an hour or two, but then I put it back before she missed it.

One day, my folks had a party in the house and I was standing at the gate onto Aldecoa Street, very bored with it all. Suddenly, I saw two or three white kids my own age playing at the base of a tree across the street. We started playing together and then they went for a walk on Dewey Boulevard. I ran into the house asking for some money, so that I could buy them some Popsicles. I bought them and then ran to find my new friends,

19

but they had gone, so I ate the Popsicles rather than let them melt.

A few days later, they came to see me and it turned out they lived right at the top of Aldecoa Street, at the corner of M.H. del Pilar. We were at the other end of the street, near Dewey Boulevard. They were the Gaylors: Boba 7, Florence 9, Billy 11 or 12, and Bob 14. I never knew what had happened to their father, but their mother ran a private school from kindergarten through third or fourth grade in their home. The school was downstairs and they lived upstairs.

When Mom found out about their school, she immediately transferred me there because she knew I wasn't happy at the Philippine Normal School. The Gaylors became my best friends and I had many good times with them. I used to sleep at their house quite often, even though the first night was very difficult for me. At home, I always went to sleep with the light on, but the Gaylors weren't having any of that, so I learned to go to sleep in the dark.

Early in our friendship, I developed some horrible sores that covered both my feet. I used to have to bathe them in some sort of purple liquid and then sit around with cloth bags over my feet so the flies wouldn't get on them. The Gaylors would take me with them by pulling me in a little red wagon until one day they told me that if I wanted to get home I would have to get out and walk. From that moment on, my feet started to get better, though they might have been doing so all along and I hadn't realized it.

Boba, Florence, and I often had stone fights with the Filipinos. There would be three or four of us and several Filipinos at a shouting distance away, and then the insults would start to fly. They would call us "White monkey" and we would reply, "Black monkey, white monkey better than black monkey." And then the stones would

fly back and forth. In one of our fights, near Fort San Antonio Abad, we were throwing mud at one another and after shouting that they couldn't hit me, one hit me right in the eye. Luckily, it was soft mud and no harm was done.

We liked going to Fort San Antonio Abad because it was a US Army post. Besides the soldiers, there was an ice-chest with a big block of ice and an ice-pick, and we could chip off chunks of ice to suck on. One day after doing this, we went up on the ramparts, and some Filipino kids lying flat on their backs on the grass and were exposing themselves to us and yelling insults. We threw some rocks at them until one of the US soldiers told us to stop because we had hit one of the kids in a delicate area.

Another day, Boba, Florence, Billy and I were going for banca (outrigger canoe) rides in the muddy river near the fort. I lost a button on my overalls and went home to have Mom sew it back on. She asked what we were doing and I told her that the Gaylors were going on banca rides. She told me that she didn't want me doing this and I told her that, of course, I wouldn't do any such thing. When I got back to the bancas, the rides were over because one of them had tipped over, and the three Gaylors had all gotten muddy and had gone home. Luckily, no one drowned for only Billy knew how to swim.

Life with the Gaylors was so much fun that I stopped missing my cousins in Germany. One Halloween, we ran around a park with sheets over us, and then lay on the grass and looked up at the beautiful stars. For Christmas, we would make long paper chains and decorate the classroom. One unpleasant memory of my days at The Little Bo-Peep School was when I told one of the kids that Mrs. Gaylor had a face like a gorilla. Sure enough, he told her and I had to stand in the corner with my hands over my head. I was so mortified.

On Sundays, I went to a Protestant Sunday school with the Gaylors. On other days, we went to the movies at the Gaiety to see the *Flash Gordon* serials. Would Flash survive the evil Ming? There was also a feature once about the Great Chicago Fire that really frightened me.

We spent many afternoons going to a two-story building housing Catholic priests that was on the boulevard near Aldecoa Street. They had the most beautiful Christmas cards with lots of angels and conquered devils on them. As a special treat, one of the priests would give us a lemon candy or two. The building was leveled during the Liberation.

When Florence's breasts started to grow, Boba and I would sneak in on her while she was falling asleep to look at this interesting development. Florence didn't appreciate it one bit and would holler for her Mom to chase us away.

One evening, Florence and I were outside the Admiral Hotel and I had a toy .45 cap pistol with me. An American came by and I told him to "stick em up." He reached for the sky and then invited us into the hotel for a dish of ice cream. Both the Admiral Hotel and the house we lived in on Aldecoa Street survived the Liberation.

The Gaylors loved my mother's cooking and I didn't. I wanted American chops and fried chicken, instead of the heavy German sauces and boiled food that we had. The Gaylors also loved all the toys I had brought from Germany and, of course, I loved theirs.

When they started to build the Admiral Hotel, right across the street from us, Mom decided it was too noisy, so we moved to a house on Maytubig Street, a small road

right near the boulevard and off Vito Cruz. At the same time, Lotte Schoenert moved to a compound of six houses across the street from us where she continued to run her boarding house.

We were still close to The Little Bo-Peep School and I continued to go there. Two new friends that I made there were Clarence and Dick Beleil. Their father was a noted newscaster who went by the name of Don Bell. I can remember hearing his name on some newscasts, but I didn't know he was Mr. Beleil. One afternoon, I went to their house to stay the night. I was about 9 at the time and we had a fun afternoon. At some time, we had put all our loose change into their little toy safe and I memorized the combination. After supper, we went to bed, and Clarence and Dick told ghost stories and said that an Asuang, which is a Filipino ghost, would come through the bedroom window while we were sleeping and carry one of us away. I became so terrified that I couldn't go to sleep. I just kept looking at the window and waiting for the ghost.

Their mother looked in on us once to make sure we were OK, and it was shortly after that that I decided to go home. I got up very quietly, crept downstairs, opened the safe, took out my money, went out on the street, and caught a small four-person bus and went home. My folks were just about to go to bed and they couldn't believe their eyes when they answered my knock at the front door. The next morning, I went to school, and Dick and Clarence were most relieved to see me. They couldn't figure out what had happened to me, and their mother was really worried when she woke up and found that I was gone. Since we didn't have a phone at the time, there was no way she could call us.

Some of my early memories of prewar Manila are:

I remember learning to cross the street on my own. I remember making the conscious decision to wait until the bus had gone far enough so that I could see if any traffic was coming from the other side of the street before crossing.

I remember going with the Gaylors to the annual US-Philippine Army parade on the Luneta and eventually going by myself.

I remember going to a U.S. Army dentist near the Metropolitan Theater who treated civilians for additional income and getting a strawberry shortcake from Dad for not crying when the dentist filled a cavity without Novocaine.

I remember Dad having an argument with a bus driver about paying a fare for me. Though I crossed the height line indicating I should pay a fare, Dad argued I wasn't old enough and he didn't have to pay for me. I knew I was old enough and didn't understand Dad. Years later, Mom told me we just didn't have much money, and sometimes it was nip and tuck whether Dad would find the 10 centavos (5 cents U.S.) to pay the bus fare to get to work.

I remember falling from a tree when a high branch broke. I was lucky that I was able to clutch the trunk of the tree, so I spiraled downward and landed on the last branch before I hit the ground. Thanks to that branch, I wasn't hurt.

I remember playing on the mud flats of Manila Bay at low tide. This was near the Yacht Club and I didn't understand why the sand was black instead of white as it was in Germany. There was the wreckage of two Spanish war ships there from the Spanish-American War and I would crawl around on them.

In 1941, they were cut up for scrap. A small section of one of their bows was still there as late as 1957. Now, that whole area has been filled in and it is the site of the Cultural Center of the Philippines.

I remember wanting a Daisy Red Ryder air rifle because it looked exactly like those in all the cowboy movies as well as like Red Ryder's of the comic books. Dad kept insisting that I get a Benjamin BB gun since it was of better quality, and he finally convinced me when he took me to a store display of various air rifles and the Benjamin really did look better. Of course, I wanted a repeater, but Dad felt it was too dangerous because you could never know if there was a loaded BB in there or not. So, I got a single shot. It lasted through the three years of the Occupation, but our Swiss border, Mr. Lienhard, had to replace the leather washer on the pump mechanism several times. When Dad died in 1962, I found it among his belongings, but regrettably I threw it away.

On Sundays, Dad liked to go swimming in the bay. We would walk out a bit on the breakwater by the Yacht Club and then swim on the side away from the club. Dad would swim and I would wade.

One Sunday, I was playing with our landlord's two boys and I decided I didn't want to go home with Dad. So, when I saw him coming I just ducked under the water, and he walked on by and went home. I played and played and had a wonderful time. Being blond and fair-skinned, I got the worst sunburn of my life. Huge blisters broke out and Mom had to keep putting some lotion on me. The smell when the skin finally peeled off was awful.

About a year later, I was getting swimming lessons from a German lady at nearby Rizal Stadium. I thought I knew how to swim a bit until another Sunday, when Dad took Frank and Peter Ries and me swimming. They were the sons of Dr. Fritz Ries and were German refugees like ourselves. Dad went off swimming, and Frank, Peter and I got a guy to take us out a little ways in his banca. Then, as we neared the shore, Frank and Peter jumped in to swim the rest of the way.

Not to be outdone, I jumped in too, but the water was over my head and I found out I was failing swimming 1A in a big way. I decided to take a big breath, sink to the bottom, and walk along until I got to shore. If I got short of breath, I would just jump up for another. Great in theory, but it was failing drastically in practice. I found that I couldn't walk on the bottom, and I was just jumping up for a breath and then sinking down, soon realizing that I wasn't getting anywhere. Just as I started to get very tired, a Filipino grabbed me and pulled me ashore. There were no lifeguards and fortunately he happened to see my predicament. I just sat on a rock next to him, thanked him very much, and got my strength back. Dad didn't see any of it and I never told him. Frank and Peter didn't either because they had gone for a walk when they got ashore.

Two or three times while living on Maytubig Street, I traded a brand new tennis ball to some Filipino kids who had these things made out of strips of bamboo, string and bottle caps that one could balance on one's hands. I thought they were terrific. Nowadays, we would call them mobiles. Dad would get very annoyed with me for trading a good tennis ball for what he called junk. None of us played tennis, so I considered the tennis ball to be junk compared with the mobiles.

In 1940, we moved across the street into the same compound of six houses where Mrs. Schoenert lived at 124 Maytubig Street. I really liked that move because there were several kids my age living there. Also, there were lovely cement driveways where you could roller skate, some nice swing sets, and some large metal animals including a deer with antlers.

Mom heaved a big sigh of relief when the Gaylors left for Australia shortly after we moved into the compound. With a mother's instinct, she felt that it extended my longevity because we always got into mischief. She never knew that there were three times when I could have been killed while playing with them.

The first time was when we walked out on some huge pipes to a dredge moored in Manila Bay that was pumping sand onto the shore. Billy, Florence, Boba and I walked out to the dredge on the pipes, which were moored on floating barges. Only Billy knew how to swim. For some reason, I wanted something from shore, so I walked to and from the shore on those big pipes all by myself. One slip and I would have drowned, but the pipes were so big the thought never entered my mind. Fortunately, I didn't fall into the water.

The second time, Billy and I went walking out on the breakwater by the Yacht Club. There was a storm and the waves were breaking over the breakwater. Of course, Billy and I went out on it and timed our steps so that we always leapt to where a wave was just receding. All of a sudden, we miscalculated and a wave swept me off my feet. Luckily, Billy grabbed me or I would have been swept off and drowned. We were both thoroughly soaked, so we went to his house and he put his shoes into the oven to dry out. His Mom wasn't home, so no one heard about our misadventure.

The third and last time was when Florence, Boba and I were making shadow figures on the wall of their bedroom during one of my sleep-overs with them. The bedroom was on the second floor and there was a street light right opposite the window. The window had a nice wide window sill that one could stand on, so it was ideal for shadow figures. The only fly in the ointment was that there was only a screen covering the large window that was taller than we were.

In the middle of our wonderful creations, Billy opened the door, saw us, and told us to stop because it was dangerous and their Mom didn't want us doing it. So, we stopped. But the minute he left the room we were at it again. Sure enough, I lost my balance and out the window I went — head-first. At the last second, Boba and Florence grabbed my legs and pulled me back in. We stopped immediately, but there was no hiding the giant hole that I had made in the screen. The mosquitoes loved it. Mrs. Gaylor was so relieved that I hadn't been killed that she didn't even scold us. The Gaylors closed their school and went to Australia shortly afterward, but the hole remained there for quite a while, plainly visible from the street.

After that school closed, Mom tried to get me into the Bordner School, but they claimed my English wasn't good enough. I then went to a very small private school run by a tutor. We were in a private home that overlooked Manila Bay, and I could look up from my textbook and see a submarine or a PT boat in the distance. There was also a beautiful, tall, older Swiss girl going to the school and I had a terrific crush on her.

Then, one afternoon, inspired by a recent *Tarzan* movie, I yelled out "Tarzan!" as I swung from the shower pipe in our upstairs bathroom. The pipe broke and a chagrined Tarzan had to go downstairs and confess.

My parents just burst out laughing and didn't even punish me.

After a few months at the private school, I started fourth grade at the American School in June 1941. I enjoyed it except for soccer practice. I could never run and kick the ball, so I was really frustrated. I did like my classmates and the little class library. Once, there was an assembly in Heilbronn Hall featuring a native band, and I recognized and hummed some tunes that I remembered from my Philippine Normal School days.

I was terribly embarrassed when our teacher, Mrs. Davis, caught me looking at someone else's paper to see if I had the right answer to a question on a surprise quiz. I had the right answer, but I had to bring the paper up to her. I got a zero for cheating.

Art class was something I abhorred. I didn't like drawing flowers or houses, so I drew tanks and planes, and got praise from the other boys in the class. The art teacher made no comment.

The American School at Calle Donada Street was about a ten minute walk from home, so I walked to and from school. In November 1941, I remember sitting with Dad on a bench near Fort San Antonio Abad and asking if we could go to America before the war came. He said no, and I can't remember if he tried to assure me that war wouldn't come to the Philippines.

Earlier, in 1940, I had a sleep-over with the Gaylors and we watched the lights of an elevator in a building across the street. Florence said that if the elevator stopped at a certain floor there would be war. Sure enough, the elevator stopped on that floor and war came to the Philippines.

RODERICK HALL'S NARRATIVE

Life revolved around family and friends. My father, a scratch golfer, was a member of the Manila Golf Club, and brought home many silver cups from tournaments. Every afternoon, we played in my grandparents' garden or with friends in the park along Dewey Boulevard, facing Manila Bay.

My mother, grandmother and aunt, all born in Manila, spoke English, Spanish, Tagalog and French. Many Spanish "Peninsulares," i.e., born in the peninsula, or Spain, did not allow their children to speak Tagalog, the dialect then spoken around Manila, now the national language. We all spoke Tagalog and changed from one language to another depending on whom we were with. My mother insisted only that we not mix languages.

Among my memories during those years is flying to Baguio in a single-engined airplane that carried about six passengers. It could have been a Beaver. In 1936, my two brothers Ian and Alaistair, and I came down with whooping cough. It was thought that sea air would be helpful, and with my

mother we took an inter-island cruise on the Mayon, a well-known steamship. In September the following year my sister Consuelo was born.

In 1937 or 1938, I was a guest at the wedding of my aunt's sister to a U.S. Army cavalry officer. The guard of honor lifted their swords and the young couple walked underneath. I well remember Ian and I being presented to Manuel Quezon, the President of the Philippines, at the wedding. It was the first time I had champagne.

In 1938, my parents, two brothers, sister and I, with our two Chinese amahs, Ah Chu and Ah Nam, went to Europe, sailing from Manila on a German steamship through the Suez Canal. My father was taken ill, and left the ship in Marseille. We continued to Southampton, and spent the summer in Edinburgh, at my grandmother's home. "Home leave," as it was then called, was usually for an extended period of up to one year. We had purchased school uniforms and had enrolled for school, but the Munich crisis caused my father to fear war was coming and he decided we should return to Manila.

We sailed to Montreal from Glasgow on an Empress Line ship, passing the SS Queen

Third grade in 1940:
Roderick Hall, Hans Walser (left, right)

Elizabeth, which had been launched and was completing her fitting out in the Firth of Clyde. We spent one month in Westport, Connecticut, with the Rudkin family in the guest house of Pepperidge Farm, their home. Mr. Rudkin, was the senior partner of a New York firm of stockbrokers, correspondents of my father's Manila firm.

Mrs. Rudkin had started to bake bread a few years earlier for her son's health, and her small enterprise became the Pepperidge Farm Bread Company. The guest cottage was several hundred yards from the main house in the middle of an apple orchard, and our amahs made apple sauce for us every day from fallen apples. I have liked apple sauce ever since. Across from the cottage was the barn where a bakery had been installed. Mr. Rudkin and my father went to work on Wall Street every day.

Our return to Manila was by train to Chicago, where we transferred to the Canadian Pacific Railroad through the Canadian Rockies, the first time I had ever seen snow. A few days later, we sailed from Victoria, on Vancouver Island, on another Empress Line ship via Yokohama to Manila. I celebrated my sixth birthday on board ship just about the time we crossed the international date line. Arriving back in Manila, I entered kindergarten at the American School.

Before the war there were few if any traffic lights in Manila. Policemen stood on pedestals in the middle of the intersections, and controlled traffic. At Christmas each year, we visited the traffic cops in front of the post office and the Jones Bridge, stopping the car in the middle of the intersection, where my brother or I handed the policeman Christmas envelopes through the car window.

HANS HOEFLEIN'S NARRATIVE

The first night that we stayed in Manila we experienced a major earthquake, which I have never forgotten. We stayed in a boarding house for a month until we rented a house at the corner of Georgia and Tennessee in the Ermita district. I went to Hoey's Kindergarten and Primary School at 1120 A. Mabini Street for a month to learn English and then started first grade at the American School in Mrs. Ryan's class. I went to the first and second grades, skipped third, finished fourth grade, and was in fifth grade when the war started.

As was typical of most of the foreign families, my family did not have much to do with the Filipinos on a social level. My friends

Fourth Grade 1940: Hans Hoeflein

26

were Americans or Germans, except for Jaime Ventura, who was a mestizo, or half-Spanish, half-Filipino.

We went on lots of excursions to Tagaytay, Baguio, Sunset Beach on the other side of Cavite, Laguna de Bay, and the hot pools at Los Baños. I remember one trip to Laguna de Bay when we went up the Pasig River by private boat to the bay. The water was dirty and brown all the way to the bay instead of the clear water that we had in German rivers.

We also went to the movie theaters, the Ideal, the Lyric, the Times and the Metropolitan. The Gaiety, which was a smaller theater, was about eight blocks from where we lived after we moved to M.H. Del Pilar across from the Apostolic Delegation and near the Malate Church. The Apostolic Delegation was where the Pope's representative to the Philippines lived in a beautiful two-story building. The Gaiety was the theater of choice for us young folks because they always had exciting serials such as *Flash Gordon*.

Life was good. Prices were cheap and we had two servants, a houseboy and a cook/*lavandera*, a *lavandera* being a washer woman. Although we had a Ford, we did not have a driver. Though we did not belong to the Polo Club, I used to go there to watch the polo games and drink milkshakes with my best friend, Joe Thomas, whose Dad was the President of the Polo Club. My folks did belong to the American/European YMCA and I used to swim in their pool. At that time, you were not allowed to wear bathing suits in the pool.

Mom and I went to the Union Church, which was an interdenominational Protestant Church, but Dad didn't go to any church or synagogue.

In 1939, we went to Nielson airport to watch the arrival of the four-engined Lufthansa plane that was to establish Far Eastern air routes from Germany, but unfortunately the plane crashed in Manila Bay, just short of Dewey Boulevard, so we didn't get to see it. Fortunately, no one was killed.

We lived near the Manila Yacht Club, so I used to hang out there and ride on the tender that would take people out to their boats. I was very impressed by the seaplane that used to be moored at the club.

In 1940, my father, Justin, was able to get his parents out of Germany. They went via the Trans-Siberian railroad to Vladivostok, then to Japan, and arrived in Manila and disembarked at pier 7. Had they stayed in Germany, they would have been part of the Final Solution.

I was a Cub Scout in Den Four Pack Three, and we used to go to Fort McKinley and do what Cub Scouts do. The parades and the band at the fort were very impressive.

Like Juergen and his friends, I occasionally got into stone fights with Filipino kids. Up to half a dozen kids on each side—whites on one side and Filipinos on the other—would hurl insults and then throw stones at one another, though in one of the fights I ended up with a split lip.

In 1941, we went to Baguio and I learned to roller skate in Burnham Park. While there, I watched a mining contest where we had a chance to see who could drill the fastest blast holes in large stone blocks. We also visited a gold mine. The drilling equipment and air compressors were made by Ingersoll Rand, the company I was to work for twenty one years later.

I had the usual toys we all played with at the time. Cap pistols, a Daisy BB gun, Monopoly, roller skates, and luck of all lucks,

27

two Lionel electric trains. My dad went to the Philippine Education store at 101 Escolta and bought me a train. At the time, they had a contest where if the last number on the receipt of your purchase matched the number that they drew, you were given the amount of money you had paid. My father won and decided to get another train, so I had a freight train with three cars and a caboose, and a passenger train with three cars. I was the envy of all my friends.

Due to the old murder charges and Dad's being Jewish, we were all deprived of our German citizenships and were now stateless. His company was forced to terminate him and they did it in a tongue-in-cheek manner. What they did was to make a deal with Mr. James Sampson, the owner of the Philippine Engineering Corporation, which was also the agent for Deutz Diesel, and so he went to work for Mr. Sampson, essentially doing what he had always done for Deutz.

HANS WALSER'S NARRATIVE

From my perspective, life was good in those early years. The American community and the Swiss community in Manila were very small and everybody knew everybody else. Social parties were frequent, as were bridge parties. My parents played bridge monthly with the MacArthurs and the Eisenhowers; Eisenhower was MacArthur's aide at the time. Servants were relatively cheap and the families in these 2 communities had several; often a cook, an amah for the kids, a housekeeper and some had a chauffeur and a laundry woman as well. We lived at 1130-B Dakota Street, a place called Dakota Court due to there being a few houses in a courtyard. Vacations for

the foreign firms in Manila were generally 3 to 4 months long every four years. When I was 4 years old the family went on a ship to the United States; had my 4th birthday in Kobe, Japan on the ship; landed in Vancouver, Canada; saw my first snow in Lake Louise/Banff, Canada; and arrived at my grandparents' house in Iowa. There I saw and ate my first candy corn. That was the only time I saw my mother's parents; I never saw my father's parents.

Life as a kid growing up in Manila was fun. We often got to attend the adult parties, since the kids were "put out to play" with their amahs watching over them. Every Caucasian family belonged to at least one club. There were several to choose from. I can remember the Polo Club, Yacht Club, YMCA and the Army-Navy Club. There were several more. We had a ritual on Sunday morning; go to church at the Union Church and then to the Polo Club for lunch and activities. There were many sport activities going on at the club and often a polo match. The men engaged in some sport but often settled down to games of liar's dice. The kids had fun times and roamed all over the place with the amahs watching over the real young ones. Yearly, a highlight consisted of watering down the polo field to a muddy mess and turning loose a greased pig, which all the kids would then try to catch (and of course, once you caught up to the pig and grabbed him, your hands would just slide off). We all got horribly muddy but there were plenty of showers to clean up. We looked forward to that yearly tradition.

Birthday parties were generally big affairs. The kids your age were invited to the parties and almost always they were the kids from the American school. There were a lot of games but the highlight was the piñata suspended by a rope from a tree that was full of shiny new centavos. The kids took turns being blindfolded, spun around a couple of times and then with a bat would take a mighty swing, hoping to hit the piñata. When it was finally hit by one of the kids, the centavos would scatter to the ground and all the kids would mob each other trying to get as many shiny pennies as they could. A centavo could buy something in those days.

One day out on a walk with the amah, we approached the Dakota Court entrance, I decided to play a game with myself. I shut my eyes, gauged the distance to the entrance and walked the number of steps to the entrance, turned left and walked right into the corner of the concrete column at the entrance. The scar on my forehead is still quite visible today.

There was one adult party that was held to savor a watermelon. One couple had taken a trip to the United States and returned with a watermelon. There was no such thing in Manila and so a few American couples had gathered for dinner, which was to be culminated with this great watermelon for dessert. At the end of dinner all the people waited anxiously to see if the taste would be as remembered. Well, the hostess had given it to the cook to prepare for the dessert and the cook, who had not seen a watermelon before, didn't quite know how to serve it. So she punctured a few very small holes in it and put it in the oven. The watermelon was then placed on a nice silver platter and brought out to the table steaming hot. You can imagine the let down that ensued.

Life for a kid growing up in Manila was good.

PART 2

LIFE DURING THE WAR

Walled City aflame after Japanese attack, December 27, 1941. Fort Santiago also hit. Luneta and Rizal Monument can be seen in the foreground. This attack was after Manila declared an Open City.

CHAPTER III

WAR COMES TO THE PHILIPPINES

JUERGEN GOLDHAGEN'S NARRATIVE

On Monday, December 8, 1941, I went to school as usual and some of the kids were talking about the Japanese having dropped some bombs near the Philippines. Our fourth-grade teacher, Mrs. Davis, told us it was just a rumor and our class continued until noon. Then, she finally admitted that the rumors were true and that they had denied them earlier because they didn't want us to become too excited in class. We were all sent home and told that the school would be closed until further notice. None of us thought that would be for five years.

Shortly afterward, we had our first Japanese air raids and we all sat in our house under an arch at the foot of the stairs to the second floor. Mr. Lienhard, our Swiss boarder, who was an engineer, had figured out that that was the strongest place in the house. So, there we sat, and I would play with some of my toys and be very scared that a bomb would come down and kill us.

The Pandacan oil tank area is dynamited by U.S. Forces preparatory to retreating to Bataan. This shot was taken from the university apartments looking east. The Agriculture Building can be seen beyond the roof of the Luneta Hotel.

33

One time, I was outside, heard some planes, looked up, and saw a flight of Japanese planes high overhead. I could see the red rising suns on their wings and quickly ran back in the house to sit under the archway. The Hinds had a beautiful air-raid shelter built of heavy beams right next to their house. I envied them their shelter and safety compared with our archway. They had recently come from the States and he worked for the International Harvester Company. At the time, I never knew the parents' names, but looking them up on a list of Americans interned in Santo Tomas, there is a Julie Diana, a Lonnie Robert, a Mildred Momson, and a Robert Hinds. (From the book *Santo Tomas Internment Camp* by Frederick H. Stevens, Stratford House, Inc., 1964, page 512.)

Robert and Julie were the two children. Robert was about my age and we became very good friends. His sister Julie was a little younger and, being a girl, wasn't much use to Robert and me. Robert had lots of fascinating toys from the States and we played a lot. After an afternoon of playing, we would sometimes get a Coca-Cola and that was a real treat for me since we never had any at home. We didn't have the money. Best of all, Robert had a Lionel train set that we loved to play with. He went to the American School with me and I remember him practicing his violin. I didn't take any music lessons.

We kids stayed mostly in the compound and seldom went anywhere because of the danger of air raids. Once I did go with Robert and his mother somewhere in their car and I remember seeing two American trucks with .50 caliber, water-cooled machine guns on them, pointed into the air. Once, at dusk, I saw a plane fly low overhead and one of the adults said it was a British Spitfire and that soon it would shoot the Japanese out of the sky. It sure didn't turn out that way.

A blackout was in effect and we had a little room where we had put up blackout paper, and we could turn a light on and read. Once, playing outside in the dark, I could see the glow of some ship on fire in Manila Bay. From one of our upstairs rooms, we could see the three tall radio towers at Cavite Naval Base and after one air-raid, there were only two of them left.

I have very few recollections of Christmas 1941. We went to Mr. Frank Swan's home, our next-door neighbor, and he had a false fireplace with some logs and a red light to make it look like there was a fire in it. I wasn't impressed, but it brought back many memories to my parents, who thought it was great. Mr. Swan was a ham radio operator, and had a large radio set and a large antenna tower in his backyard. He donated his equipment to the US Army and one day an Army truck pulled up to take the equipment. I was awed by the US soldiers.

For Christmas, the Hinds gave me half of a set of Tootsietoy airplanes and Robert got the other half. I got a red and a silver fighter and two transport planes. I played with those planes during the entire Occupation and they had many successful missions.

The annual Christmas party for the kids at the Elks Club did not take place that year. Kids would go past a long line of wrapped presents and be given one upon handing in a ticket. Years later, Mom told me that the amount one paid for the ticket determined what kind of present one got. Interspersed with the holiday season were the frightening air raids. The Hinds still had a large packing box in their garage in which their furniture had been shipped from the States. It was full of shredded paper and I thought it would be a good place to crawl into during an air-raid, but I never did. There was no way my folks were going to let me out of the house while a raid was in progress.

One day, Robert and I climbed up on the roof over the compound's garage area and when we got down, two Japanese fighters flew right over our heads. Had we still been up there, they might have strafed us for the fun of it. Since we were back on the ground, the angle of the roof hid us from view.

One afternoon, while on a city bus, I passed a field with small tents and US Army soldiers guarding them. Around the tents, I saw Japanese civilians who had been picked up and brought by the Army to this field. They were lucky in that they were only in the tents for about three weeks. When the Japanese army arrived, all Allied civilians were interned in Santo Tomas—not for three weeks, but for three years.

When Manila was declared an Open City, the US Army started destroying its ware-houses in the port area and also opened them up to anyone who wanted to take foodstuffs. Dad heard about it, went there in a taxi, and was able to retrieve some, including a case or two of V8 vegetable juice. This had come to Manila just a short time before, and Dad went wild about the taste and all the healthy juices it contained. I couldn't stand it and thought of all the things he could have brought home he had to bring home that stuff. Yuk!

A day or two before the Japanese arrived, I was standing at the gate to our compound and could see an overturned truck burning at the end of our street. I wanted to go and take a closer look, but my folks wouldn't let me. Nobody was letting their kids wander outside of the compound. Then, the Hinds and some other neighbors started burning papers. I saw some large sheets of ashes, and I could make out that they had been blueprints and I could still read stuff on them. I asked the Hinds if I should crush the ashes since no Japanese was going to

Walled City area afire during heavy raid in late December, 1941. This raid by the Japanese gained notoriety as the "Infamous Attack" after Manila had been declared an "Open City" by General Macarthur.

read them if I could help it. They assured me that the ashes would soon fall apart.

Even though Manila was an Open City, we were all afraid of what the Japanese would do once they arrived. Would they loot, kill and rape as they had done in Nanking, which had been in many papers and newsreels of the time?

RODERICK HALL'S NARRATIVE

I was in the Fourth Grade at the American School on December 8, 1941. School

The Pandacan oil tanks going up in flames. Taken from the Bay View Hotel December 29, 1941.

usually finished at 12:30, but that day my mother came to collect me and my brother Ian about 11:00. Our large seven-passenger Chrysler was full of canned gods. Dad, on hearing about the raid at Pearl Harbor, had told Mom to "go buy all the canned goods you can," which she had done just before collecting us.

A day or two later, a bombing raid sank several ships in Manila Bay. One was the ship we were booked to take to Australia in January, her next trip. Fearing the war, Dad had decided to send his family to Australia until things settled. Since Dad was not joining us, he had booked in January, so that we could spend Christmas together. I sometimes wonder if the war had started a month later whether we would all be Australians today.

My Uncle, Joe McMicking, had gone on active duty in June 1941, believing war was coming. Shortly after Pearl Harbor, being a pilot, he was detailed to fly down to Mindoro Island in a small plane to deliver a message. There he was told two Japanese destroyers had been sighted passing South of Mindoro early that morning. Instead of just reporting the news to Manila, he flew out in the direction the ships had been seen. Noting the compass direction, he estimated speed by the wakes, and then flew parallel to the ships at a safe distance to sketch their outline. On return to Manila he consulted *Jane's Fighting Ships,* and submitted his report: two British Javelin-type destroyers sighted, giving time, heading and speed. His commanding officer replied that if this had been the case, the British would have alerted them. Shortly after a message came from the Admiralty asking for information on two British Javelin destroyers in the area. This allowed an immediate response. Uncle Joe was transferred to intelligence, and sent to Corregidor. He was part of the small group to leave with General MacArthur, and spent the war as a member of his staff. He is the only staff officer wearing combat fatigues and helmet in the famous picture of MacArthur landing on Leyte.

My Uncle Alfred McMicking entered active duty with a Philippine Army Reserve unit. After the surrender on Bataan, he was taken on the Death March, and imprisoned at Camp O'Donnell, where he remained until all Philippine Army troops were released. He returned home very sick with malaria, and continued to have relapses regularly during the war.

HANS HOEFLEIN'S NARRATIVE

I'd gone to school the date of the attack. In those days, we didn't have a chauffeur, so my parents or my father would take me to school. School was from 7:30 a.m. until 12:30 p.m., with no school in the afternoon. The school was not air-conditioned; therefore we went to school for five hours, the afternoons being too hot.

When my parents came to pick me up at 12:30, I noticed that both my Mom and Dad were in the car and the back of the car was full of groceries. They had already learned of the attack on Pearl Harbor at that point and they knew the Japanese would eventually invade the Philippines. I was in the fifth grade on December 8, and the teachers didn't tell us anything about the war having started. I had no inkling of it until I saw my parents in the car full of groceries.

We lived at 1196 M. H. Del Pilar, which is one block inland from Dewey Boulevard.

The place across the street from our home was the Apostolic Delegation, which is where the Pope's representative to the Philippines lived. The Malate Church was a block away from us and about one block to the north of the Admiral apartments.

The gardens of the delegation were very spacious. The place occupied almost a city block. There was no building across from us except the delegation, which was set back from us. Our house had two stories and from our upstairs porch, we could see Cavite and its US Navy base. I think it was the next day, or the day after, that we had our first air raids on Manila. The Japanese hit both Nichols Field and the Navy base at Cavite. We could always see the three big radio towers at Cavite, which were the tallest radio towers in the world. They could communicate back and forth to the United States with them. One of the towers was knocked down during those early raids.

One day, my Dad was driving in the city and he was stopped by a US Army officer at gunpoint because the officer's car had broken down. He took our car and Dad didn't get a receipt for it, so he was never compensated for the car. A black, two-door 1940 Ford. My Dad always had black Fords.

Heavy clouds of smoke came from the burning of the oil tanks at Pandacan. We could see Pier 7 from our house and flames from the burning area. We also saw a lot of US military equipment moving north on Dewey Boulevard to Bataan because that was where they were all going. They were coming from Nichols Field and Fort William McKinley.

During the air raids, we watched from our upstairs, screened-in porch. There wasn't that much to be seen because the targets were relatively far away, such as Nichols

Field or Fort McKinley. The morning before the Japanese came into the city, there must have been thirty or forty US Army vehicles in the fields around the Yacht Club and Fort San Antonio Abad. The vehicles had all run out of gas or had broken down and were just left behind. There were no US military personnel to be seen.

HANS WALSER'S NARRATIVE

On Monday, December 8th (the 7th for the United States), I was 8 years old and attending class with my schoolmates in the 4th grade. With 4 periods remaining and the class just starting, the principal came in

Walled City bombing by Japanese raders in late December 1941. Picture from Bayview Hotel.

and quietly talked to the teacher. After talking to the teacher, the principal turned to us and stated that "School is to be dismissed right now. Most of your parents are outside waiting for you. War has been declared between the United States and Japan". Several kids left and the ones remaining left one by one as their parents came for them. The Japanese had bombed Pearl Harbor and war had been declared. I remember going out on the porch and watching the American planes flying overhead, guarding the skies. I tried hard to distinguish the insignia on the bottom of the wing to see if they were Japanese. It was exciting. Well, the planes went back to their base and landed so the pilots could have their normal lunch. The Japanese attacked at that time and caught those planes on the ground and destroyed all of them but one.

The next few days were spent between periods of normal life and periods of worrying what was going to happen next. The Japanese planes appeared often and bombs were dropping all over, especially at the pier. We all learned that when the planes came to bomb, the best place to be was on a mattress in the corner on the lowest level of the building, with your fingers in your ears and a pencil in your mouth to avoid great damage from concussion. One day I was at the YMCA club (normalcy), the Japanese came to bomb and everyone huddled on the lowest level doing what we were supposed to. I got my first "thrill" of what concussion was like as a building near-by was hit. After the bombing was over, I rushed out to see what had happened. Within eyesight was the building that had been bombed. Part of the building had been torn off and the top floors were burning. It took about 3 or 4 days before fear lost to curiosity and I was out on our porch watching the Japanese planes with a "Que sera, sera" attitude. Of course the Japanese had destroyed most of their targets in Manila the first few days and were bombing targets outside Manila. Still occasionally, throughout December, the Japanese would bomb 1 or 2 places in Manila. On December 17th, the Cavite Naval Base was bombed and we could see the smoke from the fires. The same target and same big smoke trail on the 23rd. On the 25th there was a raid on Nichol's Field. The Walled City, Fort Santiago, and Santo Domingo and the Pasig river warehouses were hit on the 27th with heavy casualties in the Walled City. This occurred after MacArthur had declared Manila an "Open City". When ammunition depots and barges were hit, we would hear the rapid fire explosions as the ammunition exploded. On the 29th, the Pandacan oil tank area was dynamited by the American forces, as the Americans did not want to leave a lot of fuel for the Japanese, preparatory to the Americans retreat to Bataan. Those fires would continue for days. Meanwhile, the Japanese Army was advancing from the south. On the 30th, American and Filipino troops were leaving for Bataan and the Japanese were nearing the outskirts of the city. The Pandacan oil blaze was still going on when January 1, 1942 arrived.

Once it had become apparent (and it didn't take long to become apparent) that the American and Filipino soldiers would be no match for a well equipped Japanese army, people were "fighting" to book passage out of Manila by plane but mainly by boat. Reservations for civilians were booked in no time and extended through December, January and February. Of course, these were mainly Americans since most of the Europeans and Chinese didn't really have any place to go. Tentative bookings had actually started earlier since it was pretty common conjecture that the Japanese would expand their field of battle sometime in the "winter".

When MacArthur made his famous "I shall return" quote, everybody in the city expected that the Americans would soon be back. A month, maybe a couple or three. No one expected 3¼ years.

TICKET TO PEACE

USE THIS TICKET, SAVE YOUR LIFE.
YOU WILL BE KINDLY TREATED.

Follow These Instructions:

1. Come towards our lines waving a white flag.

2. Strap your gun over your left shoulder muzzle down and pointed behind you.

3. Show this ticket to the sentry.

4. Any number of you may surrender with this one ticket.

JAPANESE ARMY HEADQUARTERS

降 . 票

此ヲ持ツモノ ハ投降者ナリ

殺害スル ヲ嚴禁ス

大日本軍司ハ

...our way to Peace pray for Peace

A 1942 Japanese Propaganda Leaflet
to USAFFE Troops

CHAPTER IV

THE JAPANESE ARRIVE

JUERGEN GOLDHAGEN'S NARRATIVE

The first Japanese entered Manila on Friday evening, January 2, 1942, and were well-behaved. In fact, a day or two after they had arrived Dad and I were walking up Vito Cruz toward Rizal stadium and I asked him when I would see my first Japanese soldier. Dad pointed at trucks full of soldiers that were driving past us and said, "There they are." I had thought that the men were Filipino soldiers and part of the United States Army Forces in the Far East (USAFFE).

We still had our expired German passports, so we were considered allies by the Japanese and were treated as friends. We were actually stateless, belonging to no country because our passports had expired. When Dad's had expired, he went to the German embassy in Manila and they refused to renew it because he was Jewish. Mom then decided that what was good enough for her husband was good enough for her, so she didn't renew hers either. Since I was on my mother's passport, I too became Stateless. Any Japanese who came to our house was always shown our passports and always accepted the fact that we were Germans, which was a good thing for us. They never noticed the expiration dates.

Within a few days after the Japanese arrival, all Americans were ordered to report to Santo Tomas University, with a few possessions for a three-day stay. When they realized it was going to be much longer than three days, they relied on their Filipino servants and friends to bring them bedding, mosquito netting, and anything else they needed.

A woman I met recently in our present neighborhood told me that after she and her family were interned, they asked their servant to bring them what she thought were their most precious possessions. Among foodstuffs and bedding, she brought them their family photo album. At the time, they didn't appreciate it; jewelry would have been more valuable. But time proved her right because during the Liberation their house and belongings were totally destroyed and the photographs could never be replaced.

RODERICK HALL'S NARRATIVE

Before Christmas 1941 our family moved from 1335 Oregon Street in Paco, to our grandparents' home at 740 Dakota Street (now Adriatico) in Malate. It had a very large garden, and the lot stretched through the block to Nebraska, the street behind. It was half a block from the Assumption Convent. Beyond was Ateneo, the Jesuit College. Manila was declared an open city, and all US and Philippine troops withdrawn. The Japanese entered Manila the evening of January 2, 1942. That evening, my grandfather, who had been suffering from cancer, began to fail. Dad took our Chrysler to fetch Dr Vasquez, the family doctor. He was stopped by a Japanese checkpoint

41

in Pasay that included a Japanese civilian. A soldier and the civilian got into the car, the doctor was collected, and the group returned to our home. The civilian and the Japanese soldier commandeered the car and drove it away.

Several days later, Japanese soldiers came to the house and ordered all enemy civilians to report to the Malate parish school. My mother was told that those born in the Philippines were not required to go, although my mother had become British when she married. We children hid in the maids' room during this visit. Dad packed a small suitcase and went to the school, where he remained for several days before being moved to Rizal Stadium, and then on to Santo Tomas, the Spanish University founded in 1611 that had been selected as the internment camp for civilian prisoners-of-war.

A few weeks later, my aunt Mercedes and her family came to visit. Her teenage nephew Enrique Zobel showed me some crisp newly issued Japanese occupation currency. I was intrigued, and asked if I could change some with my prewar notes. I then showed them to my mother, who told me they would one day be worthless, and made me take back my old notes.

HANS HOEFLEIN'S

only comment about the arrival of the Japanese is that what struck him most was the sight of soldiers on their bicycles. Hans and his parents went to Taft Avenue to see their arrival. There was no fear whatsoever, only a sense of curiosity

HANS WALSER'S NARRATIVE

At the end of December and with the Japanese on the doorstep of the city, my parents decided that the safest thing to do was to be with a group of people and

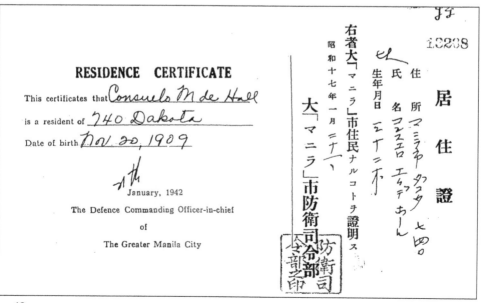

RESIDENCE CERTIFICATE

This certificates that *Consuelo M de Hall*

is a resident of *740 Dakota*

Date of birth *Nov. 20, 1909*

January, 1942

The Defence Commanding Officer-in-chief

of

The Greater Manila City

so we went and camped out at the Swiss Club. After all, the Swiss were neutral. So we left most of our belongings at home, took a few "necessities" and waited it out. On January 2nd, I can remember the rumbling as truck after truck of Japanese soldiers came into Manila. We watched from our "safe haven" as they went down the street and into the center of the city. No one knew what to expect. After all, they had ignored the declaration of an "open city". Yet we didn't expect them to be here long.

After a couple of days, the sky had not fallen and we returned to our home and hoped to sort out what life was going to be like. Changes didn't take long in coming. Our home and all the homes in the courtyard appealed to the Japanese and so we were evicted. We found a place just south at 46 Leveriza, a block away from the Rizal Memorial Stadiums. It was also a block away from the American School, which the Japanese took over. We were allowed to move our belongings. The firm where my father worked was a British firm and so closed down. My father was lucky in that he quickly got another job at a Swiss company, F.E. Zuellig, Inc. My father and I had Swiss passports but my mother was an American with an American passport and we didn't quite know what was going to happen to her. Most of the Americans were rounded up and sent to the internment camp. However, under Japanese law, the wife takes the citizenship of her husband, so my mother had a choice and obviously, she chose to remain with her husband and child. Her passport, however, stayed American.

Japanese occupation money

CHAPTER V

THE JAPANESE OCCUPATION 1942 - 1944

JUERGEN GOLDHAGEN'S NARRATIVE

SECTION 1 – STILL IN MAYTUBIG COMPOUND

Within a few days of the Japanese arrival, I woke up one morning and all my American friends and their parents were gone, having been interned in Santo Tomas. That morning, I was hanging around the large metal deer on the lawn wondering what to do with myself.

Soon, some Japanese cars and trucks drove up and soldiers were carrying some things into the first house in the compound that used to be occupied by Betty Ingram and her folks. I offered to help and carried some small nick-knacks into the house. Then, a soldier told me to come with him and took me to a bedroom on the first floor in which a Japanese officer was lying on a bed in his uniform. At the doorway to the bedroom stood a sentry with a rifle and bayonet, and I was awestruck.

Streetcars used by Japanese in 1945 battle for liberation.

The officer spoke English and asked me some questions, one of which was whether I wanted some money. Since he was my enemy, I wasn't about to accept anything from him and so said, "No, thank you." He asked what I thought about the Japanese army and I said, "It is a great army and has been victorious." Then in trying to make more conversation, I thought, "What else can I say to this man?" Well, we had a lot of beautiful flowers in the yard, so I asked him, "What kind of flowers do you have in Japan?" This enraged him and he shouted at me at the top of his voice, "What, you don't know? Get out, Get out!" and he waved his arm at me to get me out. I beat a hasty retreat, and sat on a wall across the street and wondered what I had done to get him so upset. Years later, I realized he felt insulted that I had not known about Japan.

Another day, an enlisted man tried to talk to me and gave me a silver-colored Chinese coin that I still have to this day. He had a nice smile, but didn't know any English and I didn't know any Japanese, so we didn't talk much. Mostly smiles and gestures. It was one of my first close looks at the Japanese and I thought that despite the so-called "Yellow Peril", he wasn't really yellow. He had sort of a reddish face and I guess he must have been slightly sunburned. He wore puttees around the lower part of his legs and they were very neatly wrapped. He most probably told me his name, but I never tried to remember it. After all, he was the enemy and I just wished that they would all go away and that the Americans would come back. Most of us thought they would be gone after a few months, and none of us thought it would take three years.

A few days later, I went across the street to play with the two Filipino children of our ex-landlord, a Mr. Navarro. There happened to be a garbage pile right by the house we had lived in before moving to the compound and the Japanese were dumping stuff there from the American residences in our compound. I scrounged in it and found a cardboard puzzle of small multicolored squares with small beer bottles printed on them. One had to line up the squares so that all the beer bottles were upright. It took me a while and I played with it from time to time throughout the Occupation. I believe they were Schlitz bottles.

The best thing I found were the orange Lionel cardboard boxes that Robert Hinds' train set had come in. Having played with Robert and his train set many times, I recognized them and grabbed all that I saw. According to Mom, the Hinds' servant then came to us and claimed that the train was supposed to have been given to her. My folks sent a message to the Hinds in Santo Tomas and their reply was that the train was for me.

Mr. Lienhard, an electrical engineer, got the transformer back to working condition and I had the complete working set. I played with it throughout the Occupation, though usually only on special occasions such as Christmas or my birthday because the tracks took up a lot of space on our living room floor.

The locomotive was a Lionel Model 238, a blue-grey in color, and based on the streamlined Pennsylvania Railroad locomotive. There was also a tender, a yellow-orange Shell tank-car, a green hopper, a yellow boxcar with a sliding door, and a red caboose. (When I finally came to the States in 1950 we sold it, but now I wish I'd kept it.) After the Liberation, the Hinds went back to the States and they didn't want it back.

There was a Japanese family that had moved into some new houses on Maytubig Street just before the war and they had a boy my age. A few days after the Japanese arrived, I saw him on the street and we played for a short while. We were throwing piled up sand against each other, he being the Japanese army and I the American. Since the wind was in his favor, he got the better of me. He then boasted about Japan's superior might and; while he was right at the time, I didn't like it and never played with him again.

One afternoon, Dad and I went to the Casa Mañana, which had been a nightclub that had opened at the corner of Maytubig and Vito Cruz shortly before the war. Dad took me there on the back of his bike and when we got there, there was a group of Japanese soldiers with their rifles. Dad had no fear of them, and he started to talk to them and told me to watch his bike. I had a letter opener shaped like a German bayonet, which was in its metal scabbard on my belt. To show the Japanese I meant business, I pulled it slightly out of its scabbard while looking fiercely at them. The soldiers were highly amused by this and one of them pulled his bayonet out a little too. They spoke among themselves and had a good laugh. His bayonet was a lot larger than mine and he knew how to use it. The club was destroyed during the Liberation and all that was left were two or three long pieces of horizontal concrete that had been part of the entrance steps.

Another afternoon, Frank and Peter Ries and I were sitting on top of some disabled civilian buses on Vito Cruz near Harrison Park. A patrol of Japanese soldiers marched by, and when they saw us they smiled and waved, and threw us a tennis ball and some candy as they marched by. The candy tasted sweet, but had no flavor. "Made in Japan", we thought derogatorily.

SECTION 2 – PAX COURT

On January 14, we moved out of the Maytubig compound to another compound named Pax Court, which was not too far away on Balagtas Street. Mom told me at the time that the reason we moved was because she couldn't stand the sound of the hobnailed boots that the Japanese sentries scraped on the cement as they walked night guard. (Years later, she told me that it was because the Japanese wanted our house, so that only Japanese military would live in the compound.)

The date stays in mind because the morning after we moved I came downstairs and couldn't believe my eyes at the bunch of presents waiting for me. That morning, January 15, was my birthday and in the excitement of moving, I had forgotten all about it. It was my eleventh birthday. Some of the presents had been bought on credit from H. E. Heacock, the leading department store, but we never had to pay for them. The owner, Mr. Heacock, was an American and was interned in Santo Tomas. He died shortly after the Liberation and the store never reopened.

At Pax Court, I made friends with Charles Loukes. He had recently come with his mother from Shanghai, where his family had been missionaries. I have no idea what happened to his father because he wasn't with them. Charles and I had a grand time playing together. As usual with any new friend, he had some toys I had never seen or played with and at my age that was important. Among other things, he had a chemistry set which we experimented with slightly. He also had a token for a bus ride in the States and had to explain to me what a token was. I had never heard of one. Charles and his mother were repatriated to the States on one of the exchange ships and after the war I heard that he had lost one or two fingers in an accident while experimenting with a chemistry set.

One night, as I was starting to fall asleep, there were some loud explosions and the sound of an airplane flying overhead. It was a US Army plane from Bataan making a last raid. We had hoped it meant that the Americans were coming back, but they weren't.

Every evening, we would listen to "The Voice of Freedom" broadcasting from Corregidor. One time, I heard them say that they had gotten some sharpshooters from Kentucky just like Sergeant York. I had seen the movie Sergeant York just before the war and he had beaten the whole German army, or so it seemed to me. With sharpshooters like him, how could the US lose? We had such high hopes that the Americans would be back in a few weeks or at least while Corregidor still held out. None of us believed that Corregidor would ever fall.

Along the side of our new house, there was a narrow strip of soil and I planted some papaya and corn seeds, using a large can to water them with. Sure enough, some plants started growing in a matter of days. I thought my career as a farmer was made, but we moved long before anything could be harvested.

There was also a small lawn in front of each house, and my folks would sit on ours with some of their friends. I would sit there too, and one afternoon a Japanese fighter roared low overhead and its green color scheme with the rising suns on the fuselage and wings made it look like a pre-war ad for Lucky Strike cigarettes. Another morning, I heard the loud sound of airplane engines and, on looking up, I saw several flights of twin-engined, twin-tailed Japanese bombers. They were glistening silvery in the sun

and were very pretty, and they were going to bomb Corregidor.

One day, I was looking at the movie ads in the local paper, The Tribune, and saw what I thought was an ad for a horror movie. It starred Red Skelton and though it said it was a comedy I didn't believe it, not with a skeleton in it. It wasn't until twenty years later that I thought back on it and realized that Red Skelton was not a skeleton.

Right across the street were long rows of two-story townhouses occupied by Japanese troops. How absolutely fascinating for a boy of eleven like myself, even if they were the enemy. The rear of the first floors of the townhouses, where the garages used to be, had been converted into stables for cavalry horses. These were large and beautiful horses, not small like the typical Filipino horse.

Dad always loved horses and he volunteered to break one of them in to pull a cart. I can still see Dad driving the horse down the street and thinking that he was collaborating with the enemy. Actually, Dad must have noticed that they were mistreating the horse and stepped in to help it.

Charles and I spent a lot of time wandering among the stables and mingling with the soldiers, even though we couldn't communicate with them. What we didn't realize at the time was that the Japanese love children and are very tolerant of them. One day, I was feeding one of their horses some sugar and it tried to take a bite out of my light blonde hair, probably thinking it was straw. A Japanese soldier saw what was about to happen, and stepped in and stopped the horse. Another day, Charles and I watched a soldier filling his motorcycle with gasoline and he spilled some into his eyes. It was quite painful and I felt sorry for him, even though he was the enemy.

One evening, some Filipinos and I were talking to one of the soldiers who could speak a little English. He showed us a picture of himself on a troop ship on his way to the Philippines. Then, he taught us how to count to ten in Japanese (and he did a good job because I can still do it). After that, the Filipinos started to sing "God Bless Japan" to the tune of "God Bless America". I couldn't believe my ears, but I had the good sense not to say anything, though I was very disgusted by it.

Shortly after Bataan fell, there was a whole row of US Army trucks parked on the street. Some had gashes in the hoods, but the Japanese had gotten them back into running condition. The trucks were so much more solid and well-built than the Japanese trucks I had seen.

Another time, hearing some airplane engines, I looked up and saw a four-engined flying boat, which looked rather antiquated when compared with the Pan American China Clipper that used to land in Manila Bay. The plane was a Kawanishi H6K, but at the time I had no idea what it was, other than an antique.

Charles and I found an open fuse box in one of the apartments across the street and I wondered if the electricity flowed when there was no fuse in the box. I stuck my finger into the empty socket and, sure enough, the electricity was on. I got one heck of a jolt, and was lucky I wasn't electrocuted. Never told my folks about that episode either.

One afternoon, we found part of a large American flag on a pile of leaves that the Japanese were going to burn. Having spotted it first, I took it and then we found two more sections. The only part we didn't find was the small section that goes under the stars. We kept the flag in our steamer trunk and were lucky that the Japanese never searched our house. Had they found the flag, they would have raised a lot of questions or even tortured or shot us as spies, but we had no idea. The Peters, a Swiss family that we later met in Quezon City, kept an American flag sewn into the cushion of a rocking chair.

Climbing over a wall in Pax Court took us into a driveway that led right to Vito Cruz Avenue, and across Vito Cruz was Harrison Park. Charles and I used to climb over the wall, go to the park, and look for souvenirs. We found a few American bullets and some US Army passes among some foxholes. We also came across the trailer part of a US Army gasoline tanker.

Just before Manila was declared an Open City, Mom and I were riding on Vito Cruz past Harrison Park, and we saw six or seven US Navy men armed with rifles standing in a row as they were being talked to by their leader. Perhaps they had dug the foxholes, but with the Open City status there was no fighting. The spent bullets we found may have been due to the men being nervous at night and firing some of their weapons.

Sometimes, Charles and I would wander past some Japanese supply horses in the park, but with all the horses across the street from us, we weren't too interested. Another day, we climbed across the wall and I was the parade leader, as Charles and I carried some long branches we had found and used them as flagstaffs, though we had no flags on them. Just a lot of imagination.

There was a Japanese sentry guarding the house next to the driveway we used to get to Vito Cruz, but he never bothered us. Once, I squatted at his feet and looked closely at his rifle and saw it was a US Army Springfield. I never said a word to him nor did he to me, but he never waved me away.

Everyone was trying cracked wheat instead of oatmeal and Dad brought back a sack one day. Unfortunately, it didn't taste very good and had weevils in it, so we didn't eat much of it. We switched to rolls. Another day, he brought home a large can of English toffees and those went down real easy. There was a warehouse where one could get these things cheaply in the first few months of the Occupation. We also tried Dr. Lyons toothpowder for the first time. It was cheaper than toothpaste and would go farther, but it didn't taste too good. I don't remember what we used after that.

Another afternoon, I was walking home on Vito Cruz near Rizal Stadium when a truckload of Japanese nurses stopped just ahead of me and two of them jumped off. They were all laughing and enjoying themselves, but I had a deep feeling of animosity toward them. After all, they were the enemy who had taken all of my friends away and completely changed our lives for the worse.

I was too young to have any appreciation of the Occupation being a historic event. My folks didn't have that historical appreciation either. After all, Dad had left Germany because he felt a war was coming and now the war had come to him. Furthermore, the company he had worked for before the war, J.P. Heilbronn Company, a paper and office supply importing firm, had been founded by an American veteran from the Spanish-American War named Mr. Heilbronn. He had liked Manila so much that he came back and started the company. About a year or so before the Occupation, he had sold the company to an American and had gone back to the States. Sure enough, the Japanese interned the American owner and once again Dad was without a job, but this time there was no other company to go to.

Dad then faced a problem, once again, of how to earn a living. Some rich friends told him that they knew him to be a person of good character and, to protect their money, they were willing to lend him some. The only requirement was that after the war he had to repay the loan with good Philippine pesos instead of Japanese Occupation currency. They felt that the Occupation currency would be worthless after the war because there was no gold or silver backing it. The Japanese just printed as much as they wanted and it came to be known as "Mickey Mouse" money. The friends also felt that investing in real estate was risky because no one would know what transactions would be honored after the war. So, Dad had to decide where to invest their money. Some friends told him to buy drugs because they would only increase in value as they got scarcer. Dad felt he could not make money out of other people's suffering, so he and a friend, Helmut Weigert, decided to raise animals because the Japanese were encouraging agriculture and animal husbandry. That decision later saved our lives.

To my folks and me, the sooner the Japanese were gone the better we would like it. At one time, I asked my mother why she had me tutored rather than send me to a big school like De La Salle, which was run by Catholic Christian brothers. She told me that if I had gone there, I would have had to take Japanese and they did not want me to do that.

According to Mom, our house in Pax Court was owned by a Japanese civilian who wanted us to move out after a few months so that some Japanese family could move in. My folks then decided to move to what I thought was the country, but what was really the suburbs. They were tired of having to move twice in a few months, and since Dad had decided to go into animal husbandry, we needed open fields, which were available at our new home. This was shortly after the Doolittle raid on Tokyo in April. We had heard on the radio that the Americans had bombed Tokyo, but this was played down by the Japanese.

SECTION 3 – THE GREEN HOUSE

We took a caromata, a single horse-drawn cart carrying four to six people, to the new place. It took us about 45 minutes to get there, which seemed like an eternity to me. Our new home was a green-colored house on Brooklyn Street in Cubao, Quezon City. It was a long way from Pax Court, but my friends from the city did visit me once after we arrived. Dad had a party for me and even rented a pony for them to ride on. Everyone had a lot of fun, but it was too far from Pax Court and my friends didn't come out again, nor did I visit them.

We had lots of rice paddies and open fields around us for our herd of 30-40 goats to graze in. In theory, they would produce enough nutritious milk for us to sell and make us self-sufficient. We had a large billy goat for breeding purposes and the herd would increase over time thanks to his efforts. The future knew no bounds.

We had some fine stables built for us in back of the house that were made of bamboo flooring and a framework with sawali walls and nipa roofing. Sawali and nipa are both made from palm leaves. They were nice and cool and waterproof. Weigert told me that we paid the builders about fifty centavos (about 25 US cents) a day.

Mr. Lienhard, who had lived on a farm in Switzerland, had a small holding pen made out of bamboo so the goats could be put into it and then held secure while they were being milked. He also taught my folks how to milk them because my folks had no idea.

Dad went around getting business and, according to Mr. Lienhard, he was so successful that we bought two cows to increase the milk supply. According to Helmut, Dad took a boat trip to Mindanao in the Southern Philippines to get them. Helmut thought this was incredibly brave since inter-island shipping had just started up again and one couldn't know if there would be any US submarines. While on the trip, Dad taught the German army manual of arms to some of the Japanese troops on the ship.

When the cows arrived, they had to be unloaded from a train, and one slipped off a ramp and was badly injured. She was taken to a vet, but died a few days later and was then carved up for meat. Most of the meat went to the vet to pay for his services. The remaining cow, Bessie, proved to be an excellent milk producer. Like all cows, she would try to kick the bucket over when she was being milked. I tried to milk her once just to feel what it was like, but I didn't care for it.

The billy goat was a real character that to the amusement of all us spectators used to eat lighted cigars. According to Helmut, a Japanese general dropped by one day and was so impressed by the cigar chewing that he wanted to buy the whole herd. Fortunately, Helmut was able to talk him out of it.

The billy goat did his bit and we got more goats, but quite a few died of bloated stomachs, so the herd didn't increase. Apparently, when we let them out to graze early in the morning, the grass, wet with dew, would cause their stomachs to become gaseous, then bloat, and then they would die. The vet would come out, use a simple instrument to pierce their stomachs, and let the gas out. The instrument had a sharp pointed plunger within a silver tube. Once the stomach was pierced, the tube was forced into the stomach, the plunger withdrawn, and the tube

50

would remain while the goat would spring to its feet, none the worse for wear. No anesthetic was used.

After a few visits from the vet, Dad decided that he could do this himself and he bought the instrument. Between not letting the goats graze early in the morning and the tube, we never lost any more goats due to bloat. (When dad died in 1962, he still had the instrument among his precious possessions.)

Unfortunately for us, the goats ended up eating more in feed than we earned from the sale of their milk. Eventually, when most of our customers from the non-interned community ended up being interned, we sold the herd in July or August of 1944. But then, there was also the fear that we could lose the herd to American air raids since the Americans were getting closer and closer. Since Bessie was such an excellent milk producer, we kept her until after the air raids started but then we sold her too. We needed money desperately.

Mr. Lienhard was a prime contributor to our survival because he not only paid us 100 pesos a month for room and board, but he also got a rice ration of five kilos (eleven pounds) a week from the Swiss fellow he worked for. He turned this over to us, and what Mom didn't use for cooking, she would take to the Prieurs, who lived down the street from us. They had a small electric rice mill, so they would take the rice and make rice flour. Mom would then use that to bake bread or cakes.

Paul came to live with us shortly before the war. He had been living with three other Swiss at a residence in Balagtas Street when one of his Swiss friends who was living with Lotte Schoenert boasted about her fine cooking. Paul tried to move in with her, but she had no room, so she told him about Mom, saying that she runs a good

home and is a good cook. Since we were just across the way in the same compound on Maytubig Street, Paul paid us a visit and then moved in. Paul was born in Aarau, Switzerland, on May 21, 1914, and came to Manila on April 21, 1939.

For me, life in the Green House, so called because of its color, was idyllic. In fact, it could be called life in the "Elysian Fields". We were in the country with lots of beautiful flowers, fresh air, and sunshine. Mr. Lienhard told me that because of a slight elevation, it was a few degrees cooler than Manila, which made it very pleasant.

There were lots of rice fields and open areas to roam in. Mom and Dad were home every day and I enjoyed that. In some ways, the Occupation was an equalizer for many of us. No one had cars they could use because no gasoline was available, no one belonged to any clubs where we lived, and people relied on each other for help and entertainment. One didn't have to keep up with the Joneses.

With the money and rice from Mr. Lienhard and the proceeds from the goat and cow's milk, we always had enough money. Mom and I would go to Quiapo market once a week to buy food. The market by Quiapo Church was in a huge covered shed, with numerous stalls where the food vendors would have their wares for sale — lots of vegetables, fish, rice, and meat. The meat would be displayed on white-tiled surfaces and was not packaged in any way. It was like being at a butcher's shop.

Some stalls had pre-war American food and I would look longingly at the Kellogg's cereal boxes with the pictures of promotional items. I knew that corn flakes were a luxury we couldn't afford and that unless there were something in the box itself, the coupons would do me no good whatsoever. The cereal was too expensive and we never bought any.

51

Occasionally, I would see a Japanese soldier at the market who would be shopping for his unit. I used to envy the fact that he had all the money he needed since they just had to print it. Even though he was just shopping for food, he still wore the bayonet that all the Japanese enlisted men wore.

There were purple-colored duck eggs that I thought were Easter eggs and I wondered why they had them every time we went to the market, since Easter came only once a year. They were actually baluts, which are a delicacy for Filipinos. A balut is a duck egg that is boiled just before the duck hatches so that there is a fully formed embryo inside. It is very nutritious, but we never had the nerve to try any.

Large light grey eggs were also available. They were regular duck eggs that we didn't like either. Some vendors would try to scrape off the light grey and sell them as regular chicken eggs, but after the first time we fell for it, we learned not to get fooled again.

We would get to Quiapo either by caromata or a charcoal-fed bus that was in service. We would load up the two or three bags we had that were made out of palm leaves and then go home. We did this about once every week or two.

As long as you had money, there was a variety of food available. Mom was an excellent cook and made a variety of meals using carabao meat, kidneys and chicken. For vegetables, we had talinum, pechay and okra, none of which I liked. And, of course, we always had rice or camotes. Because we also raised some hens and at least one rooster, we always had eggs.

After we sold the cow, we tried to make coconut milk, but it wasn't a very good substitute for milk. One sat on a wooden block that had a metal scrapper nailed to the end

of it. Then, one took a coconut half and scrapped the meat out of it. The scrapped coconut meat would be put into a cloth and squeezed until the coconut milk came out. It was a lot of work for very little return.

When we knew that a goat was sick and about to die, we would slaughter it and have fresh goat meat. Because all the goats were my friends and I loved them all, I could never eat any of their meat. So, Mom would fix me some chicken or carabao meat.

There is one dish that Mom made that I have never seen on a menu in the States. It was a cheap dish and was called *Lungenhaschee* or lung hash. One bought the lungs of an animal, chopped them, cooked them with some spices, and served them. It was tender, tasty, and we all liked it.

For breakfast, we had rolls and soft-boiled eggs. For lunch, I learned to fry eggs and had them with rice. Mr. Lienhard would eat all around the yolk of the egg, and then balance it on his fork and pop it into his mouth. I copied that for a while until one day I got tired of it and went back to breaking the yolk over the rice.

Since we sold our cow's milk, we used KLIM for our daily milk needs. Actually, most of it was used by me since I was still a growing boy. KLIM is a Borden product, MILK spelled backwards. It is powdered milk without the fat removed and I used to love stuffing it into my mouth. It would then stick to the roof of my mouth and slowly melt, like candy. To this day, I still buy an occasional can of KLIM and treat myself. We would put a few teaspoons in a glass, add water, stir, and there was a glass of milk. If you used a lot of powder and a little water in the glass you could pretend that the thick mixture you got was cream.

Mom was also an excellent baker. She would bake bread and, as a special treat, a cake or doughnuts. Her specialty was Frankfurter Kranz, which is a cake made up of layers, interspersed with buttercream, and then covered with a layer of buttercream and lots of caramelized sugar. It used to be my birthday treat.

Yes, I did say butter. At first, the only butter we had was canned butter that was still sold from prewar stock and wasn't very tasty. Then, when we got the cow, we had cream. Mr. Lienhard, having lived on a farm, knew how to make butter, but doing it manually was a lot of work. So, he took a wide-mouthed glass jar into which we put the cream. He then soldered some aluminum ice-cube tray partitions to the shank of an electric drill bit. This drill bit was then inserted through the screw-top of a jar by means of a hole drilled into it. A few moments of running the drill and then paddles churned the cream into butter. One had to be careful not to run the drill too long or the cream went past the butter stage. Boy, was that butter a treat!

We had lots of fresh fruit. Besides mangos and papayas, we had guyabanos and santols. Guyabano is a large greenish fruit with a spiky skin that has tasty white meat inside it. There were lots of small black seeds, but these were strained out. Santols are about the size of peaches and have a dull orange color. When broken open, they have four large seeds inside surrounded by a sweet, white, tasty pulp.

My buddies and I also ate manzanitas and duhats, which we picked off the trees. Manzanitas are a tiny red fruit. You put one to your mouth, suck out the pulp, and throw the skin away. Duhats are dark blue in color and a little bigger than a cherry. You put it in your mouth, eat the meat, and throw away the seed.

There were several families we met as a result of the milk sales. Fortunately, all lived within walking distance and soon I had a circle of friends to replace those I had left in the city. One day, I was playing on a slight rise across the road from our house and I saw a group of two women, several girls and a boy coming toward our house. Being rather shy, I ducked into the bushes and watched as they entered our house. I was then called by Mom, and I met the Wilkinson family and some other family whose name I don't recall. The husbands were away and they themselves had been released from Santo Tomas because of the ill health of the mothers. They were of British nationality.

They lived in a large two-storey green house about a 10-minute walk away on Hibiscus Road. Mary June Wilkinson, their daughter, was about my age. She was blonde and beautiful, and I had a terrible crush on her, though I never told her. Rupert Wilkinson, their son, was a little younger and we all played lots of games together. We played kick-the-can and hide-and-seek, swung from a rope tied to a tree, rode their red bike, dressed up in grown-up clothing, and had wonderful times together. They had lots of books I could borrow; one of my favorites was about King Arthur and the Knights of the Round Table.

Mr. and Mrs. René Prieur, another family, were from Chile. Chile was neutral, so the family was not interned and lived about two blocks away from us at #2 Nevada Street near the juncture of España Extension and Sta. Mesa Boulevard. Eliana was their beautiful teen-age daughter, but she was an older girl and so was of no interest to me. Their two sons, René, Jr., who was my age, and Gaston, a year younger than I, became great friends. Mr. and Mrs. Hans Peter were from Switzerland and they had a son Hans, my age, and a younger daughter, Vreneli. They lived at #5 Manga Road, right off Sta. Mesa Boulevard, about a 15-minute walk from us. Dr. Lee was a Chinese woman doctor who had a son, Johnny, who was slightly older than I, and two daughters. They lived at #2 Hillcrest, which was a compound of two to four houses on España Extension, about a ten-minute walk from us. The Greuters were a Swiss family with three daughters, one of whom, Nancy, was my age. They lived at #8 Hillcrest in the same compound as Dr. Lee.

Although my folks had not sent me to public school, they did make sure that I continued my education. They got Ms. Selma Nathan to tutor me and my friends. Initially, when we were still in the city, Mrs. Nathan had started tutoring me and one or two other kids. Then, when we moved to the suburbs, she came out and ran a little one-room schoolhouse in the Greuters' house. There were about eight of us studying there at two tables grouped by age. Mrs. Nathan also acted as my letter carrier when I exchanged letters with Charles Loukes, who was still living at Pax Court. When he was interned, we lost contact.

School was from 8:00 a.m. until noon and, as I was an early riser, I always got there early. I would sit on a stoop of cool cement waiting for school to start, enjoying the coolness of the morning. After doing this for a while, I developed some bad back pains, and we went to a German doctor who diagnosed it as a cold in my kidneys from sitting on the cement. I had to wear a warm cloth around my stomach for a while and the pain went away. From the Greuters' house, the school moved to Dr. Lee's house. Eventually Mrs. Nathan stopped coming and I went to a private class in Manila.

One afternoon, I was playing in front of the Green House when a bunch of Japanese soldiers appeared and started having maneuvers in the fields in back of the house. They had a light machine gun and went running through the tall grass and bushes, setting up their gun, though they didn't fire it. Later, when they were resting in front of

our house, one of them noticed some writing on my forearm and kept asking me if it was "name-o, name-o?" I said, "No, it is not my name, but the birthday of a friend of mine." But he couldn't understand me. It happened to be Mary June Wilkinson's birthday and I had written July 12 on my arm.

By Liberation, a year or two later, we had moved to another house but could still see the Green House. From our upstairs window, I saw an American tank firing its machine gun at the Green House and I wondered if they were firing at the same Japanese that had had the maneuvers that day.

Shortly after the maneuvers, a servant from the Wilkinsons came to our door and dropped off Rupert's red, two-wheeled kid's bike that I had enjoyed riding. The Wilkinsons had gone to Santo Tomas and wanted me to have it. It was the first bike I ever had and I got a lot of use out of it. Later, Dad did too.

After the Liberation, the Wilkinsons told us that they were sitting in Santo Tomas and heard some fire engines heading north on España Boulevard. They wondered if they were going to their house and, sure enough, they were. The Wilkinsons had let their servants move into the house, and somehow a fire started and the lovely two-story house burned to the ground.

Around this time, probably in 1943, a rash of electric wire thefts started. The Filipinos would cut the electric wires from the poles and sell the copper wire. Many people were poor and desperate for food money. It got so bad that the Manila Electric Rail and Light Company (MERALCO) announced that they would repair any breaks in the wire, but they would not replace any wire that was stolen. Mr. Lienhard rigged up an electric alarm clock with some sort of electromagnetic device that would cause the alarm to sound if the electricity stopped. One night, it went off and we immediately called the police, and the thieves fled, leaving the cut wire behind. Then, MERALCO came, repaired the wire, and restored our electricity.

One day, I saw a wasp nest on the other side of a low wall. The wasps seemed to be flying rather slowly around it, so I got a long stick and poked it. Before I knew what was happening, those wasps had flown up and given me two or three painful bites. I never tried that again.

The Japanese put on an exhibit of captured American weapons in what I believe was the old H. E. Heacock Department Store building on the Escolta. They were showing how superior they were in beating the Americans, but all I felt was admiration for the quality of the American equipment. There was a machine gun on a man-high stand with a brace on the back that one could lean against. I believe it was a .50 caliber, anti-aircraft weapon. There were also some canteens, cartridge belts and helmets. For some reason, there was also a beautiful Japanese merchant ship model on display. Finally, there was a large wall map showing the Japanese conquests in Asia. As I looked at it and saw how close the Philippines were to Japan, I saw how they were able to conquer us.

Dad had always loved horses and riding, and as a special treat he arranged for Mr. Lienhard to give me lessons. Mr. Lienhard kept two horses with us and enjoyed having company when he went riding. The only trouble was I didn't like riding, I was too high off the ground and was always afraid of falling. I fell off only once though and that was in our backyard, when the horse walked under a clothesline and I slowly went backward off of the horse's back.

Occasionally, we would go into Manila to see a movie in the afternoon. The Japanese allowed American movies to be shown as long as they weren't extolling the US Armed Forces. We really enjoyed the Nelson Eddy and Jeanette MacDonald movies. Once, I went to a late afternoon movie by myself and then couldn't find the bus stop. I asked a Filipino policeman for directions, but I just kept getting lost and ending up in the same place. Finally I phoned home and Dad had to take a bus and get me. We just managed to catch the last bus home around 8:00 p.m.

The buses were powered by charcoal, which burned in a large, round container on the outside back of the bus. The charcoal produced a gas that powered the buses. Mr. Lienhard told me the seats were full of bedbugs and he was bitten so badly he couldn't ride them. I don't remember being bitten and rode the buses.

One time, Mom and I happened upon a small store in Manila that had baseball gloves, balls, and Louisville Slugger wooden bats at a very cheap price. So, we bought two balls and two bats, and then I called up Hans Peter and asked him to meet me halfway to my house. He didn't want to come at first, but his face really lit up when I gave him a ball and bat.

Hans and I were good friends and played together a lot. He had a beautiful toy castle and knights that we spent hours playing with. Also, the Peters had a lot of books that I enjoyed reading. One time, I was up in one of their trees reading a book about the Pan American China Clipper and its trip to the Orient. A boy on the trip paid a visit to the Walled City, or Intramuros, in Manila. I wanted to take his place and fly on the Clipper to the States.

On a cloudy afternoon, after a lot of rain, I practiced my breaststroke technique in a shallow, grassy, water-filled hollow and was finally able to swim. Of course, I had no pool to practice in and we didn't live near Manila Bay anymore. My newly acquired knowledge was to come in handy after we were liberated by the Americans.

The goat herd was under the care of a Filipino, because labor was cheap and my parents felt it was too hot for me to be out in the sun. So I studied, played with my friends, and read a lot. We had a lot of pre-war magazines, including *Life, The Saturday Evening Post, Colliers* and *Good Housekeeping*. I would look them over and over and dream of the Americans' return. *Good Housekeeping* had some beautiful food ads, and I would daydream about the pies and other goodies shown. I also read a lot of books, but I don't remember their titles.

Once, Dad tried to make a pair of shorts from the hide of a dead goat. This was to have been the start of selling goatskin products. The skins were first soaked in some foul-smelling solution and then stretched on a bamboo frame. The process was garnered from various books and Dad had the shorts sewn together by a Filipino. They looked beautiful, but somewhere things had gone awry because they were too stiff to wear. They stood upright in a closet for a number of years until we threw them out. We had a lot of good laughs, but no business.

To see a military POW was a rare

sight and gave me a big thrill because it brought back to me the days of American might. I only remember it happening twice. Once, a truck drove past on a rainy day and it had lots of long bamboo poles on it, the poles reaching from the top of the truck cab to the back of the truck. Underneath the bamboo, in a space between the truck cab and the floor, were huddled several American soldiers with a Japanese guard at the back of the truck. Of course, we believed the propaganda that the prisoners were well-treated. We had no evidence to believe otherwise.

The second time, Mom, the Prieur kids, and I were waiting with other people for a charcoal-powered bus at the junction of España Extension and Santa Mesa Boulevard. A Japanese truck full of American POWs was parked nearby. There was no cover over the truck and the Americans were sitting on the floor in the rear. One of them tipped his hat at Eliana Prieur, who was very pretty, and a Japanese guard on the truck hit the POW on the head with his rifle butt. We saw it, but did not dare show any reaction. If any of the Japanese soldiers who were stand-

Destroyed during Liberation.

ing around us had seen any sympathy from us, they might have beaten us. So, while life was normal in many respects, there was always an element of fear of the Japanese. The biggest problem was that we didn't know Japanese and most of the Japanese didn't know English. And they all had guns and bayonets.

One of our family friends was Mr. Goldsmith, a German-Jewish refugee like my father. He was balding and hairy-chested and he adored me. I couldn't stand him because he wanted me to like him but I thought he was just being perverse. Just before the war, when I was wading with him in Manila Bay he tried to lift me up. I gave him a hard kick in the stomach and he let me go. I just didn't want anything to do with him. Dad was swimming nearby, but didn't see the incident.

Early in the Occupation, we heard that he had been taken to the dreaded military police headquarters at Fort Santiago. He had been visiting some Filipino friends one evening when the Japanese military police knocked on their door. They had suspected that the friends he was visiting were helping American POWs. They had the host open a safe in his house They didn't find anything at first, but then they found a secret bottom to the safe which contained IOUs from American POWs. With that, everyone in the house was taken to Fort Santiago and tortured to find out about the network of contacts. By the time the Japanese were convinced that Mr. Goldsmith was innocent and released him, he was in such bad shape that he was taken to a hospital. He died there from an infection he had received at Fort Santiago.

Occasionally, there would be a knock at our door and there would stand a Japanese officer and a soldier. We were always scared about what they could want, but they always turned out to be asking routine questions about who we were and what we were doing. We always showed our expired German passports, which satisfied them that we were allies. I was fascinated by the pistol and sword the officer always had and the long rifle and bayonet the soldier had when they made such visits.

San Marcelino church, destroyed during the Liberation.

By the middle of 1944, Ms. Nathan stopped coming to teach us, and the Prieur kids and I went to someone's home in Manila for private lessons. I think it was once a week and all I remember is studying some American geography book that had pictures of people harvesting wheat in America. Of course, anything about America was wonderful.

I enjoyed any trips to Manila, especially when we rode past Santo Tomas. At first, there was just an open fence and one could see the internees in the big yard. After a while the Japanese put up a sawali lining to block the view, but you could still catch a small glimpse of some of the internees as you went past the main entrance.

When going to the classes in Manila, we would ride a bus past a Japanese hospital that had wounded Japanese soldiers looking out the windows. They would wave to us and I would wave back. A little farther, we would go past some MERALCO repair shops, where there were some Japanese tanks being repaired. In their camouflage paint, I always thought they were very pretty. I always hoped I would see them moving onto the street, but I never did.

One day, we went to a restaurant with Fritz Mosert somewhere along the boulevard and I was bored stiff. I went outside to look at the bay. As I stood there, I heard a noise getting louder and louder, and then a tank with a Japanese soldier standing on it went roaring by. Because of the gasoline rationing, there was no other traffic on Dewey Boulevard and the tank went full speed. On another occasion with Mr. Mosert, we went to some outdoor café in mid-town Manila and, wonder of wonders, they still had bottled Coca-Cola. The height of luxury, and it wasn't that expensive either. This would have been late 1942 or early 1943.

We were still in the Green House when the Allied invasion of Europe occurred. I read in *The Tribune* that the Germans were glad that the invasion had come because now they would be able to throw the Allies back into the sea.

Section 4
Nevada Street –
Prior to the American
Air Raids

Shortly after that, we sold the goat herd. We needed money and the landlord of the Green House wanted to move into his house, so we had to move again. Dad, through his milk sales, had met Mr. Raymond, who had a wife and a young, retarded boy. He was Dutch and his wife was from New Zealand, but they were not interned because of the sick kid. Mr. Egea, the owner of the house Mr. Raymond lived in, was the mayor of Cubao and was able to convince the Japanese not to intern the Raymonds.

Mr. Egea owned four houses in a compound and, through Mr. Raymond, Dad learned there was a house for rent, so we moved there. Luckily, we had already sold the goat herd because there wasn't any room for the stables. Mr. Lienhard had only one horse left by that time and was able to put up a small stable in our new backyard. Our front yard was small and the backyard was even smaller, but the horse didn't take up much room.

Although we had sold the goat herd, we kept Bessie, the cow, for a bit longer because she was such a good milk producer and we liked the butter we were able to make. We put her in the garage and I used to have to sweep the manure away down a long driveway into the gutter. We would put her out to graze on a tether, but once in a while she would break away. We'd look out the window, she'd be gone, and I would hop on my bike and go look for her. I knew where she liked to go and I always managed to find her. Luckily, the Filipinos and the Japanese never stole her. When the air raids started, we sold her because we were afraid a piece of shrapnel or a bullet might kill her and we would get nothing.

In the Egea compound, I made another set of friends. Mr. and Mrs. Egea had two daughters, Lolita and Bebing, who were in their late teens or early twenties. Much too old for me, but both very nice. They also had a boy living with them by the name of Peping, who was a relative of theirs. He and I played a lot together, being the same age. Across from us, in the same compound, lived another family, the Carvajals. Mrs. Carvajal was the oldest daughter of the Egeas. The Carvajals had two daughters, Carmeling, who was my age, and Laura, who was about two years younger. They also had a six-year-old boy named Felito, but he was too young for me to play with.

The compound was a lovely place, with lots of trees and flowering plants as well as some bushes that grew star apples, another fruit we learned to like. The Carvajals had an ilang-ilang tree and some sampaguita bushes, which both had lovely smelling flowers.

With all the friends I had, I was never lonely. All my friends had different kinds of toys and lots of books and magazines that I could read. With that and the school lessons in Manila, I was a busy guy.

My folks even arranged for me to have piano lessons at the Carvajals' house. Their father used to work for First National City Bank before the war and then, during the Occupation, he worked for the local rice distribution board. He was very musical and I used to hear him singing songs from *The*

Desert Song with a very good voice. They had Carmeling take piano lessons and my folks arranged for me to be included. The Carvajals let me use their piano. I don't remember practicing very much, but what I really liked about the Carvajals was that they had a complete set of *The Book of Knowledge* and I would get a chance to read it before my lessons started. It contained great articles and pictures.

Fortunately for us, the Japanese were not anti-Semitic and the fact that Dad was Jewish had nothing to do with the way they treated us. According to Mr. Frank Eulau, whom I met recently, at the beginning of the Occupation a delegation of five Jewish volunteers went to the Japanese authorities to ask what their policy would be toward the Jews. They were told to go home and await further word. The Japanese then contacted Tokyo and about two weeks later got word that there was to be no ill treatment of the Jews. According to Mr. Eulau, they did classify Jews at a slightly lower category than non-Jewish Germans. I was never aware of any of this and we never had any trouble from the Japanese about religion.

Once, when Dad was in Manila, he saw two German army officers, but he didn't go near them. Not at all like Dad, who, having served in the German army in the First World War, liked the military. He used to sing German army songs when he was taking a shower. Having lost his job because of the Nazis, he had no love for anything connected with them. At that time, none of us knew what was happening to the Jews in Germany, but it was a good thing that Dad didn't approach the officers.

Dad's whole philosophy during the Occupation was to keep a low profile. American friends of ours had asked us to keep a chest of their possessions when they were interned. We readily agreed. When we got it, Dad went through it and found a large photograph of someone in a US Army uniform and he burned the picture. At the time, I thought he was being silly, but he was right again. If the Japanese had ever searched our home and found it, we could have been considered to be aiding the US Army, and we knew what had happened to Mr. Goldsmith.

Neho Prieur, whose real name was René, but we all called him Neho, was my best friend. Dad always loved Wild West stories, and I read a lot of cowboy and Indian books. The height of a relationship among the Indians was to be a blood brother, so one day Neho and I became blood brothers. We each cut one of our fingers with a pocket knife and then pressed the bleeding cuts together, thus mingling our blood. His brother, Gaston told us we were crazy to do this, but I think he was jealous. Once, he became very angry at me when I found a rosary entwined with a copper necklace and a medal or two on the road going to their house. I gave the whole thing to Neho and nothing to Gaston.

One of the many great things that the Prieurs had was a collection of *Popular Mechanics* and *Popular Science* magazines in bound volumes that went back several years and right up to December 1941. One of the issues had a story on the US Navy with a large cover headline, "Second to None". How ironic.

Their house had a large backyard and a high wall around the house and yard. From the outside, only the roof of their house could be seen. Separate from the main house was a long two-story structure, the lower half a garage and above it the servants' quarters and a room where they kept the magazines. The ground floor had a cement walkway around it covered by vines and was always nice and cool.

In the back of the yard, they had a stor-

age area where they had all sorts of car parts and assorted stuff. Mr. Prieur had worked for the Ford Motor Company and must have been an engineer. One time, he had a car engine taken apart in the cellar of their house and he was trying to explain to us how it worked. I was only interested because we had never had a car and I had hardly ever ridden in one. Neho, Gaston and I would rather have been out playing, so the lesson was a failure.

One of the cars I did get to ride in occasionally before the war, was one belonging to Mr. Martin Ekstrand. Mr. Ekstrand was a co-worker with Dad at J.P. Heilbronn Company and, being an American, was interned at Santo Tomas and later at Los Baños. Mr. Ekstrand was a diabetic and always needed to get insulin. In August 2000, I attended a reunion of the Bordner High School Alumni in Tucson, Arizona. The Bordner High School was a great competitor of the American School in Manila. Although I hadn't gone there, I went to the reunion to see if I could locate friends of mine who had attended the school. I didn't find any, but on the last evening I met a man who had been interned, first at Santo Tomas and then in the Los Banos internment camp. I asked him if he knew Martin Ekstrand and he said Martin was his closest friend and mentor throughout their internment, both in Santo Tomas and Los Baños. He went on to remind me that Martin had a bad case of diabetes, but while in Santo Tomas, Martin had a German friend on the outside who would smuggle insulin in to him. So, before going to sleep at night, Martin was able to give himself a shot of insulin. I was proud to say, with tears in my eyes, "That man was my father."

Neho, Gaston and I used to wander through the fields looking for termite nests. These were about four to five feet high and made of dried mud. They were really hard and we used a crowbar to break them open and then a shovel to get at the queen ant and her special nest. We would then kill her and the termite nest would die, which is what we wanted.

I rode my first carabao with Neho and Gaston. A local farmer let us take turns riding it, which was easy because it had a very broad back. It was also much lower to the ground than a horse, and I felt comfortable and confident. Since they don't have sweat glands, carabaos have to take a mud bath one or more times a day. So, they were quite dirty and, though we sat on a cloth, I did develop a rash of sores on my thighs. So, my carabao riding career ended after the first ride.

On two or three days, the Prieurs and I looked out from their servants' quarters and saw a large, white Japanese observation balloon at a distance. It was tethered and never moved, so we lost interest very quickly. We never saw it again once the air raids started.

As we got hungrier and hungrier, Neho and Gaston started fishing for frogs. They had bamboo poles and string, and then they would dig for worms, which were easily found. They would thread the worm onto the string, tie the worm into a loop, and cast it into the water. It was messy putting the worm on the string and I took no part in it. They would fish in a concrete foundation of a large house whose construction had been halted by the war. Since it was full of rainwater there were lots of frogs. The frog would grab hold of the worm and wouldn't let go as it was yanked out of the water. The next stop was the frying pan. They smelled delicious, but I never tried any.

My attempts along the food line were to grow eggplants and batani beans in our front yard. I used a hoe and dug through the grass to turn up the soil. The eggplants grew fast and well, but I never liked them.

The batani beans grew on a vine like wildfire and were very good. Mr. Lienhard had some flower boxes in his front window and grew tomatoes. None of this was enough to make us self-sufficient and fortunately we were always able to buy some food. Even so, we kept getting hungrier because there wasn't that much food to buy. The news had more and more articles about the possibility of American air raids and how to build air-raid shelters. So, all the men in our compound got together and dug out a shelter in the central front yard and covered it with heavy wooden planks and soil. It looked very nice, but none of us ever used it because it filled with rainwater and had some green worms swimming in it. I still continued my piano lessons, but no longer at the Carvajals. I had to go to the piano teacher's house, which was several blocks away.

RODERICK HALL'S NARRATIVE

While Juergen was having his experiences in the suburbs, we continued to live in the district of Malate. Several months after the Japanese arrived, we had a visit from two Japanese who had been my grandmother's gardeners. They were dressed in suits and ties, probably part of the civilian administration. They were friendly, and had a gift for my grandmother, and candy for the children. We kids were not very nice, and after they departed, threw the candy away. For several months after the occupation, our Chinese amah, Ah Nam, dressed in a regular dress, not the usual black pajamas and light blue top, to make her look like a Filipina, because local Chinese had heard of the Rape of Nanking, and were afraid.

We attended St Paul's Girls' Convent School, run by a French order of nuns. Boys were allowed to attend until the sixth grade. Japanese language lessons were mandatory. The nuns were a few lessons ahead of us and did not seem to care if we cheated, so we whispered answers to each other. We learned the katakana script, and developed a simple knowledge of the language. This came in handy later, when I spent several army leaves in Tokyo, and could read station signs in katakana.

I was at school when Tojo, the Japanese Prime Minister, visited Manila. Every school was asked to send a delegation of students to the Luneta Park, between the Manila Hotel and the Army and Navy Club. There was a large grandstand for the dignitaries, and the crowd of students stretched back to the Rizal Monument. Everyone was given a small Japanese flag, and had to bow and shout "Banzai" when told. I thought this was exciting, but on returning home got a real scolding from the family for having participated.

After sixth grade, which must have been late 1943 or 1944, we were tutored at home by an Austrian couple, Dr and Mrs Modry, refugees from Vienna, where Dr Modry had been a professor of mathematics. They had been given shelter by the Jesuits at the nearby Ateneo. My brother Ian and I were tutored daily in mathematics, chemistry, physics, botany, zoology, English and French. I still remember it as great fun. Dr. Modry took us into the garden to examine flowers and plants for our botany lessons; for zoology we watched the slaughter of the pigs raised at home. Dr Modry showed us all the internal organs, and explained their functions.

Once a week Ian and I went to the Malate Church for catechism class with about ten other young boys and girls. Malate Church was run by the Columbans, an Irish order of priests. We were taught by Father Monahan, a balding man with glasses about forty years of age. Father Monahan sat at one end of the table in the refectory, and would light a big black cigar, that he smoked as he taught us our lessons. I remember him fondly. The church was the site of a massacre during the liberation of Manila, and all the priests and those sheltering with them were executed there.

My grandmother's large garden was turned over to raising a wide variety of vegetables and fruit. Avocados, over 150 banana trees, mangoes, eggplant, tomatoes, camote, etc. all thrived. Grandmother and I made many trips to the nearby Bureau of Plant Industry to get new kinds of vegetable seeds, and for advice. We monitored the forty or fifty hens daily, and those not laying were destined for the kitchen.

During the early years Dad managed to get many passes from Santo Tomas to visit us at home. Some passes were a month long, and he had to periodically check in. All prisoners on release wore arm bands with Japanese characters to denote their status as civilian prisoners of war. This Dad usually hid with a coat he carried over his arm. He was often given free rides on the horse drawn calesas, the only public transportation. As the war progressed, he would only get a few half day passes. All leaves finally ended.

In 1941 Dad was 38 years old. As a young man without family in camp, he was assigned to work as an orderly with the elderly men, most soldiers from the Spanish-American war, 1899-1901, who had settled in the Philippines. Single men were housed in the gymnasium, with beds head to tail in tightly packed rows. For a time those who were very ill and could not care for themselves were transferred to an island in the the Pasig River, connected to the Ayala Bridge. An insane asylum occupied most of the island; the old men were kept in a building at the far end. We occasionally visited

Dad there, walking past the building where the inmates were housed. A family friend who was an inmate shouted at us from her window, always remarking how much we kids had grown.

While on the island, Dad, a senior orderly, had to report weekly to camp on the status of the elderly men. He would arrive at the front office of Santo Tomas, throw his raincoat over a chair and enter to make his report. An internee orderly would take the raincoat to hang, and while doing so would remove the cash that was stuffed into the pockets. This cash represented funds raised outside to help the prisoners' committee to bribe the guards for extra food. This was repeated weekly, and fortunately the Japanese never caught on.

We went to play on Dewey Boulevard almost every afternoon. There was always a group of children there, including British friends given passes to live with friends of their parents. Each week we went to the movies at the Gaiety Theater, a local flea-bag. Action serials were shown before the main feature. We chose to go on the day they showed both the old and new serial.

On the corner of Dakota and Herran streets, half a block from our house, there was a four- or five-story apartment building with a veranda on the main level, about five feet off the ground, because of the danger of floods in the area. It had been requisitioned by the Japanese for a comfort house for officers. The veranda was partitioned into dressing rooms. Ian and I, with friends used to hide in the bushes outside, and watch the women in their slips, put on their makeup. This fascinated us. Most of the women looked Chinese or Korean. One day, drunk sailors stopped us and made rude signs to show they were looking for women, so we directed them to the officers' establishment.

Almost no one worked during the war. Af-

ter Uncle Alfred was released from Cabanatuan prison following the signing of the peace treaty with Japan, with his friends he organised a weekly poker afternoon at home. The group arranged with my brother Ian to provide and serve refreshments. Ian would go to the markets and bargain to buy cakes, etc. and cigars and cigarettes for the group. His profit was the difference between cost and what they paid him. This became a profitable sideline for Ian, particularly the cigarettes. Ian regularly bargained hard with the old women selling cigarettes, some weeks turning over five or ten thousand cigarettes, selling at retail to all who wanted to buy from him.

Grandmother's home got quite crowded, and eventually there were three or four people sleeping in each bedroom. Marita Lopez Mena, a family friend, had her house requisitioned by the Japanese, and moved in. There were five adults, four children, the housekeeper and amah sleeping in the house. Six servants slept in rooms over the garage. Every day my aunt Helen's fiancé, Carlos Perez Rubio, came to spend the day. In the rainy season, when it flooded, he'd ride over on one of his polo ponies. Before the war the Perez Rubio brothers had their own polo team. On a few occasions strange men visited Uncle Alfred, and spent the night. They were usually gone by morning. Were they guerrillas? I was too young to know.

An outing I remember was the day we all went with our Ortigas and Ramirez relatives to spend the day at the beach in Paranaque. Without cars, and the beach quite a distance away, we hired two calesas, small horse drawn carts. Everybody piled in, and off we went. It was a wonderful day, although I got a sunburn. We kids were often barefoot.

Many well to do people suffered financially during the war because their funds were held in branches of US or British banks, all closed during the occupation. Those working for foreign companies were not paid, those working in import/export had no business to transact. All my father's accounts were in banks that closed. Fortunately, my great grandmother, Josefa de la Madrid, living near by on Nebraska Street, kept her accounts at the Bank of the Philippine Islands, that remained open throughout the occupation. She survived the war, carried by her chauffeur on his back across the lines to safety in mid February 1945, and she died in 1953, over 100 years of age.

As a child I was not aware of any hardships nor lack of food, but it was a fact. We have the letter Mom wrote to Dad in Santo Tomas that said "Do you remember the diamond brooch you bought for me in Paris? I sold it for a 2-kilo can of dried milk for the children."

HANS HOEFLEIN'S NARRATIVE

Like Rod Hall, we continued to live in the city. Shortly after the Japanese occupied us, we could see their bombers taking off from Nichols Field, or Nielsen Airport on their way to drop bombs on Bataan and Corregidor. Occasionally, we could see clouds of smoke over both places.

In March or April of 1942, the schools re-opened. My parents then enrolled me at La Salle and I used to walk there. Most of the students were either Filipinos or mestizos. There were very few Caucasians at La Salle. I don't think there were that many Caucasians living where we were because most of them had been Americans or British, and they'd all been interned by then.

When the Japanese started interning the Allied people, many of our neighbors were Americans and some were very good friends of ours. Several of them left their belongings with us for safe keeping, but unfortunately their belongings were all burned along with our stuff during the battle for Manila.

I remember Mom and I going to Santo Tomas many times in the first two years to take in food and things. We would get notes from our interned friends as to what they wanted and we would try to bring it to them. There was a big shed where the outside people could meet the internees and give them what they had asked for.

Of course, the Japanese would watch what was going on and they would either search the package or just let it go through. You had to be careful you didn't put in any contraband because you never knew which ones they would search. During the first couple of years, there were some places where Filipinos were bringing things that belonged to American military prisoners of war at Cabanatuan or Camp O'Donnell. These were things like cartridge belts and military insignia, which they would offer in exchange for sugar and things that the prisoners needed. I ended up with some small pieces of military equipment because we knew that what we gave for those things was taken back to the prisoners. We had heard from the Filipinos who were trading in those goods that all those military prisoners were on a starvation diet.

We also had a lot of visits from Japanese propaganda people to the school when we had assemblies. I have always thought that these people were trained in the United States because they spoke fluent English. They would talk to the students about how much better the Japanese system was than the U.S. system and how lucky the Filipinos were to be part of the Greater East Asia Co-Prosperity Sphere. Once a Japanese officer, speaking perfect English, told us that American soldiers fighting the Japanese greeted each other with the slogan "Kill a Jap." We took this to be pure propaganda because how could he have known? The favorite slogan of the Japanese was "Asia for the Asiatics."

About four or five times, they assembled the whole school and give us Japanese flags, and we had to stand along one of the main roads like Dewey Boulevard or Taft Avenue waving our flags whenever some Japanese dignitary would come to town. They would then use this to make propaganda films of the enthusiastic Filipinos welcoming their benefactors.

There were two Japanese victory parades that I remember. One was on the Escolta, the main shopping street in Manila, and they had a lot of captured American equipment, some American prisoners, and some Japanese tanks, besides the marching Japanese. I also remember that because we lived across from Dewey Boulevard, after the surrender of Corregidor in May of 1942, they landed the American prisoners by ship at Dewey Boulevard and had them march up the boulevard to Bilibid Prison. By coincidence, I spent most of my adult career working for Ingersoll Rand and got to know one of the engineers who had been in the US Army on Corregidor and participated in the march up Dewey Boulevard. We always commented we must have been within twenty to thirty yards of each other at that march.

Besides our usual classes, we also had to learn Japanese or Nippon-go. This was taught by a Brother Leo, a Christian Brother, and not by a Japanese. Being kids, we would frequently say at school, "Nippon-go, American come." But we made sure we never said it within the hearing of a Japanese.

Most of my playmates at the time were Spanish or mestizos, namely half-Spanish and half-Filipino. One of my best friends, Jaime Ventura, was Spanish and was later killed during the Liberation. Of course, Liberation didn't become a common word until the Americans came back and we had been liberated. During the Occupation, we all used to say, "After the war."

At the time, I did not have any strong feelings toward the Japanese, one way or the other. During the first years of the Occupation, the Japanese tried very hard to win the Filipinos over to their side. Of course, that meant to their way of thinking and culture, and the majority of the Filipinos just didn't buy into it. They wanted the American way of life back. I do know that other than the piece of ground that a Japanese soldier stood on, the Philippines was only occupied by the Japanese where there was a physical Japanese presence.

I did not see any atrocities committed by the Japanese during the Occupation, though from time to time I would see some Filipinos tied to telephone poles and just left there. They were still alive when I saw them. I assumed that they had been thieves who had been caught in the act. I never saw anyone shot or beaten.

Of course, you had to bow to a Japanese sentry whenever you passed by and if you didn't you would be called and slapped across the face or beaten more severely depending on the mood of the sentry. I did get slapped once by a sentry. I don't remember if I didn't bow at all of if I bowed too quickly, or perhaps not deep enough. Whatever the reason, while I may not remember the why of it, I do remember the end result.

In 1943, I went by myself to the Paco Railroad Station and caught a train for a ninety minute ride to visit some friends in San Pablo. I had been given a piece of paper in Japanese identifying me as a German, but I did not carry it with me on the trip nor was I asked by anyone about my nationality. While there had been many Japanese visible until the fall of Corregidor, after that and until early 1944, there was not a highly visible Japanese presence. I stayed in San Pablo for about a week and then took the train home.

Toys were a luxury that we didn't get, so a group of my friends and I used to make model airplanes on our own. Mostly we made models of Japanese or American planes. Since we couldn't get balsa wood we would make them from pine wood or wooden boxes. We drew up plans from various magazine pictures of planes. We made our own airplane glue from celluloid film that we got from somewhere. We would take our mothers' nail polish remover, which was acetone, put the film in that, and presto, we had glue. We also made our own paints.

Until the Japanese confiscated all our cap guns, we used to run around a lot with them and play war. We didn't have any caps, but vocal noises sufficed. We also had battles with slingshots, but instead of stones, we used paper wads. With our roller skates and golf clubs, we had field hockey games. On Sundays, I went to the interdenominational Union Church with my mother. And so, we did what kids do and waited for the Americans to come back.

We used to go to the Yacht Club and wait for the Japanese to come by boat from ships in the harbor, and we would buy cigarettes from them and then sell the cigarettes to Filipinos and make some money for ourselves. We would yell, "Ohka tobacco, ohka tobacco," which meant that we wanted to buy cigarettes. Two of their brands were Akebono and Pirate. The Pirate brand had a picture of a pirate on the pack.

About two houses away from us were the Sequia Apartments, which were occupied by Japanese naval pilots. They were quite friendly and many spoke good English. When they left in late 1944, they left the apartments and garages unlocked, and we went in and found all sorts of small airplane parts. I remember taking a piston as a souvenir. Thinking of those pilots reminds me that we would frequently see two-seater, orange biplanes performing maneuvers in the air. It turned out that these were training planes and were the only planes with that color scheme.

Fortunately, all this time my father continued to work and bring in enough money. Dad had been working for the Philippine Engineering Corporation, which was the Deutz distributor for the Philippines. Deutz, a Germany company, made diesel engines. They had a large machine shop in Manila and the Japanese took over the shop. Mr. Sampson, the owner, asked my Dad to run the place in his absence, since he was interned in Santo Tomas. There was a very nice Japanese civilian, Mr. Funabiki, who taught me Katakana, and even in early 1943 was convinced that Japan could not win the war.

In 1943, Dad convinced the Japanese that they could run the shop better than he could because he really didn't want to work for them. So, then he went into business with another gentleman, and they started converting trucks and buses to run on charcoal, and that's what they did until the end of the Occupation.

In 1942 or 1943, the Nazis in Germany contacted the Japanese and asked them to return my father to Germany because he was considered a murderer by the Germans. Fortunately, the Japanese had too many other things to worry about than returning my father to Germany. I don't remember how my Dad found out about that, but he did tell me about it.

From 1942 until 1944, I went to La Salle. One of the things the Japanese introduced while I was still there was calisthenics. They called it Radio Taiso and we would exercise to the instructions coming over a radio loudspeaker. Whenever a high-ranking dignitary came to Manila, we schoolboys were given small Japanese flags of paper and had to go to Luneta and wave the flags and yell banzai. We had to do this two or three times. Toward the beginning of 1944, the Japanese kicked us out of the La Salle building and I ended up going to Santa Scholastica, which was originally a girls' school run by nuns.

By that time, we also knew that things were starting to happen. The Americans were getting closer and the Japanese military was starting to increase in numbers. Although we had a radio, it had had its short wave components removed. The Japanese required that all radios be brought in and have the short-wave coils removed. Once that was done, you had a certificate to put on the entrance to your house and also a paper was pasted on the radio to certify that it had been de-short-waved. This was a requirement and if you did not do it and they found out, you were taken to Fort Santiago for torture, or toward the end, you were executed.

Some of our friends retained their short-wave radios, listened to William Winter on radio station KGEI from San Francisco and, by word of mouth, we could gather what was happening with the course of the war. Of course, the Japanese published an English newspaper named *The Tribune* and there was KZRH, the Japanese-controlled radio station. These told only the Japanese version of the news and that the Allies were constantly suffering horrendous losses and defeats.

Transportation was becoming more and more difficult. There were pre-war streetcars, but they were only on certain fixed routes. There were also horse-drawn carriages. These were two-wheeled with either a caromata, which could carry up to four or six people, or a caretela, which carried two or three people. Also, a new industry sprung up in the form of the pedicab. It was a bicycle with a single seat in the usual place for the driver, and a two-wheeled contraption in the front in which one or two people could sit. There were some charcoal-powered vehicles, but no gasoline-powered buses. Gasoline was only available to the military and to high-ranking government officials.

Until the American air raids started in September 1944, we always had enough food. We had lots of rice, vegetables, and carabao meat. My mother would make cottage cheese from carabao milk. She had a big sack hanging in the kitchen in which she would let the milk curdle. The water would drip out and in that way she made cottage cheese. She also made sauerkraut from green papayas. Our refrigerator was a Servel and, before the war, it ran on gas. Then, my Dad brought someone in who converted it from gas to electricity. I guess electricity was cheaper.

We had two female servants. One was the house girl who did the cooking, the dishwashing, the cleaning, and other things around the house. The other was the *lavandera* or washer woman. My mother did the food shopping and would take the girl in charge of the cooking and walk to the markets. There was a small market near us and they did not go to the major Quiapo market because that was across the river from where we were and too far to walk to.

Every once in a while, we would go to the Escolta, the main shopping street, and also to a movie there because the Gaiety was not air-conditioned. The movie houses on the Escolta were the Capitol and the Lyric. Once we even went to an operatic production at the Metropolitan which was near the Post Office.

Behind us were the Michelle Apartments and one of my friends by the name of Toda lived on the top floor. My friends and I would go up to his apartment, which faced Manila Bay, and we could see all the ships in the bay and also all the way to Nielsen Airport and Nichols Field.

Around August of 1944, the Japanese kicked everybody out of their houses if their houses fronted on Dewey Boulevard. This even included the Apostolic Delegation. They didn't occupy the houses, but just wanted them emptied. We were not kicked out at that time because we were one block inland. Interestingly enough, the Japanese did not kick the people out of the Michelle Apartments, even though that building was the tallest one in the area. I had a key to the Apostolic Delegation grounds and I would go there and watch what was going on. Since there were no Japanese in the building, I would go up to the second floor and have a great view of Dewey Boulevard. I was lucky I was never caught, as they could have treated me as a spy. By that time, the Japanese were becoming very tense about the progress of the war.

HANS WALSER'S NARRATIVE

Life for me as a kid was pretty boring. Most of my friends from school were Americans and were interned in Santo Tomas. My father still could go to work but my mother no longer taught at the University of the Philippines. My parents decided that I should not go to public school. They did not want the indoctrination that would go on. At various times the kids would all be marshaled out for parade and have to wave a tiny paper Japanese flag. Students had to learn Japanese. With my mother being American,

that just couldn't happen. So I was home schooled by my mother. With my mother being a math teacher and with me growing up in the Orient with a European father and an American mother, math and geography were a snap. My mother did a good job as when we were repatriated in 1945 to the United States, I took several tests to determine what grade I should enter, and I entered the grade that I normally would have had I continued on at the American School.

We continued to have one servant, Valentina, who was in her late teens or 20, and our "all duty" gal. She lived with us through the entire Japanese Occupation. My parents' social life was quite curtailed, as there were no more Americans for parties and bridge. However, there were other Swiss and Europeans (mainly Spanish and Germans); enough to still have some parties and bridge groups. The Swiss Club helped to maintain some kind of normalcy and was a rock for us. To pass the time, my mother who was an outstanding bridge player, taught me how to play bridge at the age of 8, and my father taught me checkers and chess. So the next few years I played a lot of those games. At the beginning of the occupation, the Japanese had killed my piano teacher so that ended my time on the piano. There were only a couple of kids in my neighborhood that I spent time with, Billy Conn and Roy Filer. Roy was a few years older than I was but he was right across the street and he didn't have many kids to play with either. Roy survived the retaking of Manila but Billy did not. Charles Loucks, who lived near me and was also a playing friend of Juergen for a while, was a close friend. He was often called Schumel, a name I think he brought from when the family lived in China as missionaries. He and I were introduced to chemistry sets and we enjoyed messing around with them. This was in the early part of the occupation. We made gunpowder and often would put the powder in a container and blow it up. We also made nitroglycerin. We would dilute the nitro, put it though a small hole in a piece of balsa wood the shape of a cigar, attach small tin fins to the rear, wind up the fins with a rubber band and position it at one end of the bath tub. The "torpedo" would zoom over to the other end of the tub and explode (a very small explosion that barely made a sound). Schumel, as Juergen relates, lost a couple of fingers a few years later doing something with his chemistry set. Anyway, I lost him as a playing friend when the Japanese decided that he and his mother should go into Santo Tomas.

City life in Manila under Japanese occupation was as normal as could be. Wherever I went, I either had to walk or go by calesa. My father was not allowed to drive his car. The Japanese had all cars stay off the streets to save gasoline. Only a few car owners were given special permits. So transportation was either by streetcar or caleza. I do not remember what happened to the car but I believe it was confiscated by the Japanese. I do remember it not being in the garage.

The Japanese did not want chaos; they wanted to show how good they could be and there was no way they wanted to maintain control over a chaotic situation. The Filipino money was replaced by Japanese Occupation money and that was used for all transactions. You were not allowed to have any American dollars or Philippine pesos. Old American movies played in the downtown theaters—Jeanette MacDonald and Nelson Eddy; *Flash Gordon*, etc. The selection was small and English was the one language that the population could understand. At that time there were not a lot of Filipino movies that had been made.

As the occupation wore on, medicines became in short supply and everyone worried whenever anyone was taken ill. I remember putting my foot into an old shoe that was in the garage only to be stung by a scorpion. I was in great pain and the swelling was huge. The remedy was staying in bed and waiting it out. After several days, I finally recovered. Another time I was swinging on a rope in the garage, when the rope broke and I fell several feet with my head hitting the concrete floor. I became delirious from that and when I woke up the next morning, I found myself strapped to the mattress in my bed to keep me from falling and hitting my head again. Towards the end of the occupation my knee got hit with a piece of shrapnel. The doctor, Dr. Eulau, removed the shrapnel and poured sulfur over the gash simply to close it. I remember more about the disgust and criticism of me, that I had been hit and needed the scarce medicine, than anyone caring about me. One time Mrs. Case across the street developed some sores on her arm that got heavily infected with pus. The only cure available at that time was to put leeches on to suck the pus out. Looking at the arm with the leeches became a vivid memory for this young kid. When the infection was cleared, the only way to get the leeches off was to take a match to her arm and burn them off; also a vivid experience that I was allowed to watch.

Likewise, as the occupation wore on, food got scarce. So called "luxuries" were no longer available, or if they were, not affordable. Instead of toothpaste for brushing my teeth, I had to use cigar ashes from my father's cigars. For calcium we used to grind up egg shells, and put them in fruit juice and drink it. We ate rice in various forms at each and every meal. We ate a lot of coconut and got a lot of our milk from the coconuts. The Filipino lechay (spinach) was our main vegetable and camotes (sweet potatoes) were added many times to fill us up. For a while in 1943 and 1944, I had several chickens that I took care of. We were very happy to get the eggs and during a very bad flood November 19th and 20th in 1943, we had to bring the chickens upstairs onto our porch. However, they developed a disease and had to be burned without us getting one piece to eat. I also had a pet goose, Admiral, my pride and joy. The day came when we had to eat him, and I remember declaring that there was no way we were going to kill him. Sobbing, I took him in my arms and climbed onto the roof so that no one could get him. Valentina, climbed up onto the roof and as I tried to get away, she grabbed him by the tail. With him squawking loudly, I could bear it no longer and Valentina brought him down to the kitchen and killed him. That night everyone but I enjoyed the rarity of goose. There was no way I could eat any part of my pet. I will talk more about food later.

The Japanese did not trust the people. A Japanese-sponsored government of Filipinos was established but the Japanese were still leery and watchful for betrayal from Filipinos, but definitely from Caucasians. There were several random searches of our house from time to time and occasionally, but rarely, they would just take something. My father had a short wave radio that he would listen to at night. Where he hid it, I never did know but the Japanese never found it either. If they had, I'm sure that would have been the end of us. Every night at 11:00 he listened to Chungking and New Delhi. Then he would go over the next day to the Case Compound and talk to Mr. Walford, a Britisher, who listened to London at midnight. My father knew when the Americans had landed at Lingayan Gulf and closely followed their march toward Manila.

Every so often, we learned of people being taken to the Fort Santiago to be interrogated. Some were friends of ours. Some came back okay; others came back severely beaten; and others never were seen again. You never knew who or when someone would be dragged off for questioning and why it happened. On rare occasions, the Japanese would catch some Filipino who had committed some "crime" against the Japanese. In our area, that person was brought in front of the Rizal Stadium, one block away, to be held up as an example of what happens to someone who crosses the Japanese. The soldiers would gather the people in the area to witness this. Three times I was unfortunate to be among the gathered people in the area and witnessed one having his eyes pried out; one having his testicles beaten by a club; and one being skinned alive.

I, along with many others, often played a deadly game. When you were out walking and came to a Japanese soldier, you were required to bow before passing. Certainly you had to do this when you came to a sentry. If you didn't bow, you could be beaten and even killed. Well, you didn't want to bow so if you saw the situation coming up further down the street you were walking, you crossed the street so you didn't meet the Japanese soldier and didn't have to bow. The Japanese knew this is what you were doing too, and so sometimes you would be called over and hit anyway. So the mind game went on any time you were out walking; what is the situation ahead, and if a problem, just when did you cross the street without making it obvious.

The Japanese soldiers were everywhere, as was the Japanese flag. The soldiers liked to tease you by jabbing you with the point of a bayonet, not hard and not enough to hurt you. They just seemed to get a kick out of it. The officers would occasionally show their authority by hitting or slapping civilians. This did not happen frequently. Some of the officers were privy to what was really going on in the war and knew of American progress. They became meaner and more suspicious of everyone. Searches of your home became frequent. They watched you very closely, especially the Caucasians. People started getting picked up and put in trucks to go out and work in the airfields to make dummy planes. More and more Filipinos were drafted into becoming spies on their own people. There was an alley near our street that we called "gangsters alley". Two of these spies happened to go in there one night to get information. The next morning they lay in a marsh—dead. More and more people were being picked up for questioning. A friend of ours, a very nice guy about 50, was taken in for questioning. He had recently discharged his servant because the servant had tried to steal some things. The servant went to the Japanese and said that this man lived in an American-owned home (most of these had been confiscated when the Japanese first came). Although this wasn't true they took him to Fort Santiago. There he took quite a beating but he came out alive, which was a rarity for anyone who was taken to Fort Santiago at that time. I saw him about a week later. His eye was patched with a bandage and his back was cut to ribbons. Most of the people taken to Fort Santiago were never seen again.

One time, my friend Roy Filer, who lived diagonally across the street, and I went out to the airbase in the southern outskirts of Manila. We went to log in the times of arrival and times of departure and what kind of plane it was. We were on a spy mission!!! I was 11 years old. Roy had initiated this trip and I remember creeping up through the bush with him to silently watch the proceedings. It was then I discovered that the Japanese had built a lot of dummy airplanes that were parked at various places on the field. I think they were made of cardboard and were placed there so that any American plane that came would use up their bombs to destroy these "planes". We stayed for a few hours and then went back home. As I look back on that day, what a crazy thing to do! If we had been caught, we certainly would have been killed and perhaps even tortured. And since my parents didn't know what I was doing or where I had gone, I just would have ended up missing. Ah, the

recklessness and immortality of youth.

The Japanese soldier was a very proud person. He considered himself a cut above any of the civilians. He could take what he wanted from you and no questions dared be asked. It was not uncommon to see a soldier's arm laden with wrist watches. They seemed to get a kick out of accumulating as many as they could, so you would see six or seven watches lined up on the soldier's arm. Many wore glasses. Most were quite short. Many walked around with the neck flaps on their caps hanging down. For many years after the war I could not tolerate seeing that cap. Japanese civilians or veterans wore it, just like kids and grown-ups in America wear fatigues. The soldiers talked in a very staccato high-pitched loud way. Many Japanese were quite bowlegged. Some looked quite funny. And that was another problem. If you laughed at a soldier, or even smiled at something you thought was funny, you were almost sure to be beaten. I learned very early to laugh internally and was quite good at not exhibiting any emotion outside. That trait remained with me for years and years and to this day I still do not laugh loudly. You always were very wary of any Japanese soldier because you could not predict what would set him off and what he would do. You blended into the background whenever you could. But they were impossible to avoid whenever you went somewhere, because you generally had to do it on foot and there were Japanese most everywhere. I became non-confrontational, another trait that remained with me for decades.

The newspapers were a constant source of information. The Tribune published all the normal stories of everyday life, the same as before. The parties made news with who was hostess and who attended. Weddings continued on and were reported. Sports were a big thing. And of course, the Japanese triumphs on the war front were front page articles. The paper was littered with propaganda. There was no doubt that the Japanese were winning the battles everywhere. These were broadcast on KZRH and in the newspapers. But my father, with his short wave radio, knew what was really going on. Word had it that the Japanese had landed on the west coast of America and were proceeding inland. One story in the paper described a battle between Japanese airplanes and American ships. After the Japanese plane had dropped all his bombs on the American ships, the pilot dove right into the side of an aircraft carrier. The force of the hit and the explosion of ammunition on the ship, caused the plane to be blown back out and upward. The pilot, realizing his opportunity, then dove down hitting another carrier. Both sank. Another story had a Japanese aircraft pilot engaged in a dogfight where he did quite well. However, he ran out of bullets so he sped home. Unfortunately, two American planes took up the chase, one plane directly behind him and another plane just below that. Both were shooting at the Japanese plane. Having no bullets with which to defend himself, the pilot grabbed the rice cakes he had in the cockpit to snack on, and threw them over his shoulder at the pursuing plane. The rice cakes hit the American pilot right in the eyes. He lost control of his plane and flew downward, hitting the other American plane. Both planes crashed as the Japanese pilot continued home. These were actual stories in the widely circulated daily newspaper.

The house next door to us, on the south side, was owned by a Chinese. It was a big house with a big back yard. The Japanese confiscated it. Lt. General Wachi, Director-General of the Japanese Military Administration and Chief of Staff of the 14th Army, took up residence there. Every day he had a routine to go to "work". His cadre of foot soldiers would get a beautiful white horse ready. The general would then mount the horse and make his way through the streets to his headquarters. A "jeep" of soldiers

would follow behind slowly. On one occasion he took the time to talk to my parents. He described the war with sadness. He had gone to college in America and liked the Americans very much. But, as he put it, he was Japanese and he would do whatever it takes for his country. However, he was responsible for having an air-raid shelter built in the front yard. This consisted of a thick corrugated steel semi-oval that was entrenched in the ground, with about 3 feet sticking out above the ground and about a foot dug out in the ground. No one knew at the time, that this was to be of great use to us in the future.

About July 1944 the Japanese took the streetcars off and transportation became very bad.

Flash!! Americans had landed in Leyte. This was the news my father got listening to his illegal short-wave radio. That made everyone feel a lot better for we felt that our ordeal would soon be over.

Manila City Hall

PART 3

THE LIBERATION

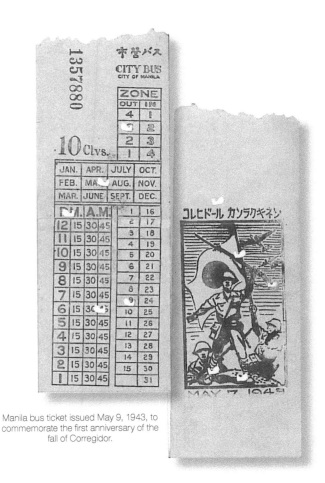

Manila bus ticket issued May 9, 1943, to
commemorate the first anniversary of the
fall of Corregidor.

CHAPTER VI

THE AMERICAN AIR RAIDS 1944-1945

JUERGEN GOLDHAGEN'S NARRATIVE

Thursday, September 21, 1944, started off like any other day during the Occupation. I went to my piano teacher's house and I can remember seeing a low-flying Japanese fighter taking off from the airfield that was near her house. That was a lot more interesting to me than the piano lesson. As I sat at the piano, we heard a loud explosion and the whole house shook. We didn't know what it was because there had been no air raid siren, but we immediately crawled into a narrow space between the ground and the floor of the house as more blasts shook the area. I was really scared, but kept my eyes open, and at a distance I could see two planes flying in a circle, chasing one another. It wasn't like a dog-fight in the movies where planes zoom up and down, so after a moment I glanced aside. When I looked back, the planes had gone and I guess one of them got shot down. They were too far away from me to be able to tell which was American and which Japanese.

At last, the Americans had returned. Happiness filled my heart after the all-clear siren. I could see huge clouds of black smoke at a distance. Being very happy, I whistled a song as I walked along. I stopped at the Prieurs' house, which was on my way home, to share the good news. They told me they had heard someone whistling and

The Sta. Cruz/Binondo area, with Binondo Church in the background.

asked if it was me. I said, "Yes, it was". And they said, "Are you crazy"? I asked them why they said that and they replied, "You are walking past all the Japanese out there who are mad as wet hornets, and you're whistling a happy song. Do you want to get beaten up or killed?". So, I went the rest of the way home without whistling.

Mom had been at her sewing machine when she heard and saw lots of planes flying high overhead and told Dad, "It's an air raid, the Americans are back!". Dad told her that they were Japanese planes on maneuvers because *The Tribune* had written the day before that if one saw a large number of planes in the air not to be alarmed because the Japanese air force was going to have maneuvers. It wasn't until they could see the planes diving down over Manila Bay with anti-aircraft firing at them that Dad was convinced that Mom was right.

The first three days of the air raids, we huddled under a shelter that Mr. Lienhard had built in our living room out of a large breakfront and some other furniture. It was very narrow inside, but strong and had room for the four of us. We sat on a mattress with a cork on a string around our necks. We would put the cork in our mouths as the explosions drew near because somewhere Mom or Dad had read that a large explosion could cause you to bite your tongue off. I also had an aluminum pot over my head and wished I was a soldier, because they had strong helmets.

When our neighbors heard about being in our shelter, they told us they all watched the raids because they knew the Americans wouldn't bomb civilian targets and it was so interesting to watch the show. So, we never went into our shelter again and just watched the show. That was a lot less frightening than cowering in the shelter.

And it was a great show. One time, we stood outside on our second-floor porch and watched several hundred silvery, single-engine American carrier planes winging their way over our house to Manila Bay at a high altitude. Flight after flight passed overhead and filled the air with the roar of their engines. One plane nose-dived and plummeted all the way into the ground. Later, we were told that it had been a Japanese fighter.

After all the planes had passed overhead, the anti-aircraft guns started and we went inside because of the danger of falling shrapnel, which one could hear falling on the roofs. Several times, I found small metal fragments on our driveway with very sharp, jagged edges.

Once inside, we no longer went into our shelter, but sat at Mr. Lienhard's upstairs window and watched. Mr. Lienhard told me that one day when he was on the upstairs porch watching, a Japanese soldier shot at him. He missed and Mr. Lienhard quickly went back inside. After that, we didn't go out on the porch anymore.

At first, I couldn't figure out what the emblem was on the American planes. It looked like a white circle surrounded by a black circle. It wasn't until one flew low overhead while I was visiting the Prieurs that I saw it was a white star in a black circle with white bars on each side. The pre-war insignia with the white star and the red circle in the middle of the star was gone. The red circle looked too much like the large red circle on the Japanese planes.

Life was not so normal anymore. No more piano lessons and no more private tutoring. I could still go to the Prieurs and the Peters and, of course, I played a lot with the Egea and Carvajal kids. Mom and I did not go to Quiapo market or any other market. Mom had noticed some women go by our house early in the mornings with food in their hands. They were going to the local market to sell it, so Mom bought food for us from them, and we no longer had to worry about going out and getting caught in an air raid.

One morning at breakfast, we heard two planes fly low over the roof of our house. A few minutes later, the air raids sirens went off, but we already knew. Usually the radio would announce, "Attention listeners, attention listeners, this is an air raid. Please inform your neighbors," at the same time the sirens would sound.

I didn't recognize the new American planes, but the P-38 with its twin booms was instantly recognizable and beautiful. Once I saw two of them dip out of some low clouds and instantly go back into them. There was no air raid alarm and I just happened to be looking in the right direction. On another clear day, I looked up and saw a lone P-38 flying high overhead and glistening silver against the blue sky.

Peping and I were playing in his backyard one morning when we heard the rapidly growing roar of

engines, and a twin engine A-20 attack bomber flew by so low that we could see the pilot in his cockpit. It was having engine trouble and looked like it was about to crash. I ran into our house to the kitchen window and saw a lot of Japanese running across the fields in the direction the plane had gone, but it didn't crash. After we were liberated, the Prieur kids met the pilot whose unit was stationed near their house and he remembered that flight.

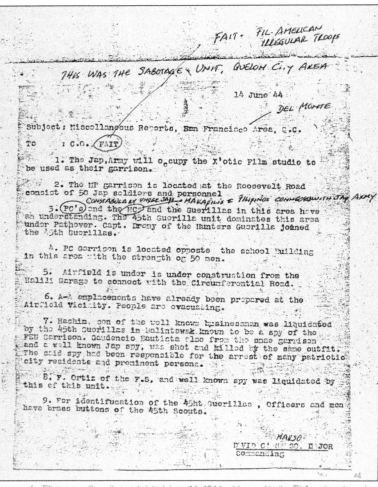

A copy of a Filipino guerilla unit report dated June 14, 1944 addressed to the Fil-American Irregular Troops (C.O. FAIT), which was a sabotage unit in the Quezon City area where we lived.

One early morning, I was standing just outside our front door when two Japanese planes flew past at a very low altitude. Suddenly, an American plane started to dive down on them, and I ran into the house and made for the kitchen window. When I got there, the planes had gone. There was no air raid alarm. Now, I wish I had stayed and watched the action, but at the time I was really terrified because I thought I could get killed by a stray round. (And I have since read that several people did get killed that way, by a piece of shrapnel as they were standing by an open window watching the action.)

Once, I was on our front lawn when an American plane appeared, diving toward nearby Camp Murphy. Puffs of white smoke trailed from its wings and then I heard the sound of its machine guns firing. I immediately ran into the house. Though these were frightening episodes at the moment of occurrence, I never suffered any lasting effects in terms of nightmares or being traumatized. After all, I wasn't physically hurt by any of it and the Americans were our friends. How could they hurt us?

Three of us were playing on the street in front of our compound when a silvery B-25 flew low over us. We never heard it coming and we were lucky that they weren't strafing anyone or we would have been killed. Most probably, they were looking for trucks or columns of troops.

I remember only two instances of seeing American planes shot down. The first was a single-engine plane that had been shot down by anti-aircraft fire. Half of the rear tail elevator had been shot and the plane spiraled downward like a falling leaf. I did not see any parachute.

Occasionally, we would see flights of B-24s, majestic as they flew overhead. We could hear the rumble of their bombs, which were still terrifying though they were dropped at a distance from us.

On January 8, 1945, Mr. Lienhard and I were watching a formation of B-24s being shot at by anti-aircraft when one of them started to trail a thin line of white. I told Mr. Lienhard that I thought it was a contrail, but he said, "No, it's on fire." Just before it disappeared from our view over our roof, it burst into flames and came tumbling down. I don't remember seeing the fuselage, but there were plenty of long flaming orange streamers coming down against the blue sky backdrop, as well as a slowly falling burning wing. There were three to five parachutes, and later we learned that the Japanese used them for target practice and none of the crew survived. Although the plane appeared to be over our house when it burst into flames, it fell quite a distance away in San Juan. Strips of shiny tin foil came fluttering down and some landed nearby. At the time, we couldn't figure out what they were, but now I know that they were metal strips that planes would release to confuse enemy radar.

We didn't have air raids everyday, and on those days I could go out of the house and play with my friends. During an air raid, we all stayed in our houses and I don't recall any when I wasn't at home, except for the very first one. It also seemed like most of them started no later than 10:00 AM. There weren't too many Japanese planes in the air anymore, especially when there were hundreds of American planes in the air. One of the Japanese planes did roar by low over my head while I was standing in the backyard of the Prieurs. It was beautiful with the large rising sun emblem on each wing. It was so low I could make out the wheel-retracting panels on the underside of the wings. Several afternoons, when walking home from the Prieurs at about 5:00 p.m., there would be a single Japanese fighter flying high overhead and I could make out the rising sun emblems on the wings. It was a pretty sight against the sky.

Outside the Prieurs' house, there were a few native huts and a large stand of bamboo trees hanging over the street. One day, to our surprise, there was a Japanese fighter being repaired under the bamboo stand. We were all fascinated by it and would watch them for hours working on the plane. After they finished the repairs, they would hand-crank the engine to start it and then the plane would taxi on the streets to the Circumferential Road, where it would take off. It was always late in the afternoon when they took off, but I never got to see this.

One time, I did see the pilot get in and one of the soldiers put a bunch of bananas in a little hatch in the back of the plane. One of the planes had an unusual design in that it had a cockpit for the pilot and another small cockpit right in front of the tail. I have since looked at numerous pictures of Japanese planes and have never seen that type.

At the time, I wished I knew Japanese so I could understand what the soldiers were talking about, but I didn't and neither did any of my friends. None of our parents wanted us to learn it. The Japanese repaired several planes there and fortunately for us they were never attacked by American planes.

Shortly after the landing of the Americans in Leyte, the Egeas showed us a leaflet that they had gotten. It showed the landings in Leyte and we all gawked at the new type of helmet the American soldiers were wearing. We thought they still had the World War I version that they had had in 1941. The leaflet also had MacArthur's "I Shall Return" pledge on it and the observation that indeed he had. Of course, if a Japanese had found the leaflet in our possession we would have been shot, so we quickly looked at it and then it was hidden from view.

As the Americans came closer, we heard about cases where the Japanese would herd all the Filipino males into a church, and then burn down the church and machine-

Destroyed buildings on Dewey Boulevard. Luneta Hotel on the left.

gun the survivors. Also, that some Filipinos would work for the Japanese with bags over their faces while they pointed out anti-Japanese Filipinos, who were then tortured and shot. The fear factor of what the Japanese would do when the Americans came closer was increasing.

One evening, my Dad came home very upset and Mom asked what had happened. Dad had hired a pedicab to take him home and the cyclist wanted a bigger tip than Dad had given him. Dad told the guy off and walked away. Mom was horrified that the man would go to the Japanese and tell them we were spies, and we would be taken to Fort Santiago and tortured. Fortunately, nothing happened.

Someone informed the Japanese that two sons of a farmer living on our street had guns buried in the front yard. The Japanese found the guns and shot the two sons on the spot. Dad and I used to walk farther down our street to another farmer to pick up some carabao milk because we had sold our cow some months earlier. Right nearby, under some trees, were two Japanese gun-hauling tractors. How I wished I could signal the American planes that they were there and have them bombed, but there was no way for me to do it. Also, there were many times I wished I could get a ride in the cockpit of one of the American planes and get a ride back to their base and be free. And, of course, get candy and chewing gum.

One morning, I came downstairs to breakfast and my parents said, "Take a look outside." There, in front of our house, was a pile of ammunition in plain wooden boxes clearly visible from the air. They were piled as high as I was, about 5'6", and I could see more piles in front of the Carvajals' house as well as other piles farther down the street, some in front of empty lots.

The Japanese believed that the Americans wouldn't bomb the ammo in front of civilian houses, and fortunately they were right. I don't remember having any air raids about that time, and two or three days later the boxes were covered with light green tarpaulins, not camouflage-painted in any way.

Edgar Krohn, Jr, a friend of mine living in Manila, recently sent me a copy of a Filipino guerilla unit report dated June 14, 1944 addressed to the Fil-American Irregular Troops (C.O. FAIT), which was a sabotage unit in the Quezon City area where we lived. The report was extremely detailed about everything the Japanese were doing in the area. From that, I assume that American intelligence must have known about the plane repairs and ammo piles on our street. Thank goodness, they didn't do anything about it.

Then, we learned that the Weigerts had been moved from their house so that the Japanese army could move in. The Peters were told to leave their house because it was on high ground and it was going to be fortified. The Peters were intending to move in with us and I was delighted, but the day they came over to talk to us about it, the Japanese put a notice on our front gate as well as the gates of several other houses. When the Peters saw that it was similar to the one put on their house, they thought we would have to move as well and they didn't come. Instead, they moved to the house of Mr. Gutierrez, who lived about a twenty-minute walk from us. I visited them once or twice with my parents and I ran around on the top of a large air raid shelter they had in the backyard. It was covered with dirt and unless you knew where it was, you wouldn't notice it. Later, that saved their lives.

Two houses to the left and across the street from us was where a Japanese machine gun unit had moved in. Later, they told us that the signs on our gates stated that the houses were reserved for them, so that other units wouldn't move in. I guess they didn't want to run the risk of being bombed if there were too many Japanese living too close together. Whatever the reason, we were delighted that we didn't have to move.

Then the Japanese used our driveway to repair some cars that they had converted into pickup trucks. I used to watch them and was interested in the colorful knobs

Manila City Hall, 1945.

that they put on the steering wheels. I had wanted one, but there weren't any extras and I never asked. Much later, I learned that they were necking-knobs. They were putting them on to make it easy for them to drive with one hand if they had to. Again, luckily for us, the Americans never tried to strafe the trucks.

The machine gun unit men became friendly with us, and Mom would invite them in for

a cold drink of water once in a while and also let them keep a bottle of water in our refrigerator. It was a used General Electric with the round cooling unit on top and we had bought it just before the war.

One day, one of the soldiers came in with a large fish, and made signs and noises. Mom thought he wanted to put it in our ice box, but he finally got the message across that it was a gift for us. We were very grateful and Mom told me it was particularly generous because, by then, the soldiers didn't have that much food either.

One of the men was a medic and always carried a large bag with a Red Cross symbol on it. I believe his name was Mr. Sato and he spoke German, so we could communicate with him. We all liked him and he would come over in the evenings and chat with Mr. Lienhard and my folks. They would talk about family life and the progress of the war. Unfortunately, we never wrote down his name and address.

Once, one of the Japanese brought a bottle of sake over for Mom and Dad to try. I was there for the grand opening and Mom was very skeptical. She said, "It makes a nice sound pouring out of the bottle, so maybe it'll be all right." After trying it, she said it had no real kick to it. The bottle had a yellow label on it, but we couldn't read Japanese. Still, it was nice of them to share.

In a partly completed house about a block away on New York Street, there were some other soldiers. We had nothing to do with them, but in the mornings we could hear them shouting and doing calisthenics. I was too scared to go near them, though we could watch them from our kitchen window.

Fortunately, on a day when Mr. Lienhard and Dad stayed home, we learned that the Japanese had confiscated all bicycles ridden on the streets that day. For some reason, they didn't take them from us in the house as the bikes were in plain view inside the front door. I guess those who came to our house considered us to be their friends, and they had the cars they worked on in our driveway, so they didn't need the bikes.

Dad still had to go into the city occasionally to buy and sell things to make money, so he used the kid's bike that the Wilkinsons had given me. He figured correctly that no Japanese soldier would be seen riding on a kid's bike. Once, I watched Dad ride it and I had to laugh as he rode away from me with his knees sticking out to the sides as he pedaled.

Later, Dad told me that he had ridden the bike into the city once and exchanged some Japanese occupation money for pre-war Philippine pesos. Everyone knew that the Japanese currency wouldn't be any good once we were liberated, but if the Japanese caught you with it you could be sent to Fort Santiago for torture to reveal the source, or just shot. Well, Dad hid his in the handlebars of the bike. Sure enough, on the way home he had to pass a Japanese control point, and had to get off the bike to explain who he was and what he was doing. Luckily, they didn't search him or the bike because after all he was a German and their ally, but one never knew what the Japanese would do.

One day, as I was walking past the ammo piles on my way to the Prieurs, one of the Japanese soldiers working on one of the piles stopped me and asked as he pointed at me, "Amerikano?" I replied: "No, Deutsche". He then said: "Deutsche, Japon, tomodachi neh", meaning that Japan and Germany were friends. I smiled and nodded affirmatively and walked away, thinking we're anything but friends. (When I think back on it now, he was just another human being trying to be friendly and I have to admire the technique he used.) At the time,

being a teenager, I didn't have any friendly thoughts toward him.

I was in the Egeas' backyard one evening and I could hear some Japanese voices on the other side of the Egeas' back wall. I looked over the top and some Japanese were sitting on a bench eating in the dark. One of them saw me and offered me some raw fish they were eating, but I declined.

One morning, one of the soldiers came into the Egeas' yard, called me over and, with gestures, demonstrated how to play a little game with him. We stood a short distance apart with our palms nearly touching each other. We would then push our palms against each other in short jabs, trying to make the opponent lose his balance and move one of his feet. One could use force by slapping the palms hard, or feint and move one's own palms aside so that the opponent would lose his balance as he pushed against the air. I enjoyed the game, but I was a little afraid. After all, he wore a bayonet as they always did. We played the game for a few mornings and then he stopped coming.

Neho, Gaston and I used to cut grass with a small, hand-held, wooden-handled, curved knife. We would tie the grass into small bundles and sell them to the horse owners for about five centavos (2.5 US cents) a bundle. We didn't make much money, but we got to know some of the horse owners. They used the horses to pull carramatas or calesas.

Anyway, they would let us ride their small Filipino horses bareback and I was really proud of myself. Just like an American Indian. When I told my folks about this, they put a stop to it. They were worried that if I fell and broke any bones, there was no way to get me to a doctor to set them. The American air raids played havoc with any transportation.

One afternoon when I got to the Prieurs, Neho and Gaston asked me if I wanted to see a hanged man. With some hesitancy, I said yes and they took me up the stairs of the garage and told me to look. From there, you could see out over the fields to a distant road, but I couldn't see any hanged man. Then they said "Look down." When I did, I saw a clay sculpture of a man's head with a rope around it, hanging from one of the wooden beams of the garage. Some joke! They laughed and laughed, and I was relieved. The clay head had been done by one of their servants and was really a fine sculpture.

Christmas 1944 was pretty barren for presents. I don't even remember what I got, but there wasn't much money to buy things and there weren't many toys available other than local stuff made out of wood, which I disdained. Furthermore, there weren't any stores nearby and the air raids made travel hazardous.

Previously, we had always managed to have a Christmas tree, using a green pine-like tree that we had growing in the front lawn. We would unearth it, put it in a pot, move it inside, and then replant it after Christmas. With the homemade air raid shelter in the living room, there wasn't any space for the tree. So, we decorated the breakfront with Christmas tree lights, covered it with a white sheet to look like snow, and put the few presents on top of the sheet.

On Christmas Eve, we opened them and Mom got a small bottle of Chanel No. 5 and two or three pre-war American cigarettes. They were Chesterfields and so old that they had brown spots on their white paper. Still, they were American cigarettes. We kept the presents on the break-front for a night or two and, on one of those evenings, a Japanese soldier who we did not like paid us a brief visit. Whether you liked them or not, you never refused entry to a soldier. After his visit, we noticed that the perfume and cigarettes had disappeared.

We knew he had taken them because he was the only outsider who had come in, but we were too afraid of what he might do to us if we reported him, so we didn't.

What was left of the business district.

On or about the same Christmas Eve, we heard a plane fly low overhead. It was an American plane and had dropped some leaflets bearing MacArthur's Christmas wishes. Dad had gone outside and seen some, but he didn't bring any into the house. Sure enough, a little later there was a knock on the door and a Japanese officer asked if we had picked up any of the leaflets. We were able to truthfully answer "No" and he went away without coming in.

Soon, it was January 1945, and the Americans were getting closer and closer. One afternoon, one of the soldiers visiting our house saw a map we had open to the Philippines and its surroundings and, pointing to Halmahera, an island near the Philippines, he said, "Takusan Takusan Amerikano, no good ja-naika." He meant that there were many many Americans there and that was no good. We agreed and wondered when they were going to reach us.

At the beginning of the war, we had stocked up on a supply of canned goods, such as evaporated milk, KLIM, corned beef, and others, but as the years passed the supply grew smaller and smaller. We thought that with fighting coming we might have to flee into the fields, so Mom sewed some rucksacks for us out of some sturdy drapes that we had. We were ready to put our remaining larder into the bags and take off into the fields.

The closet had a drawer in it that I opened one day and saw some gold-colored wristwatches with metal watch bands. What were we doing with those watches? Knowing I shouldn't have found them, I never dared to ask Mom or Dad at the time and later forgot all about them. I thought they might have been given to Dad to raise money for the guerillas. Helmut Weigert told me that they might have been given to Dad by people who wanted to sell them, but were too shy to do so themselves. Then Werner

Deutschkrohn told me that his father and my Dad had formed a joint jewel company named Godeco. That was most probably the reason the watches were in the closet. While Mr. Deutschkrohn, a German refugee like ourselves, had started a very successful sausage factory during the Occupation, Godeco was formed too close to the Liberation to have time to succeed.

One day, Dad decided to go and check up on the Peters' house. Dad had his expired German passport, so he felt that he had complete freedom of movement. We went to their house and spoke to the officer in charge, who was very nice and could speak German. They had not done anything to the inside of the house as far as we could see, and Dad reported it to the Peters. I did see the officer's cap lying on a table and wanted to ask him if I could have it, but I was too shy. From what I have learned, it was a good thing I didn't ask. If he had given it to me and if our house had been searched for some reason and the cap had been found, we would have been shot or at the very least severely tortured. How could we have gotten an officer's cap unless we had killed the officer? Besides, I am sure that possessing any part of a Japanese army uniform would have been illegal. Despite my stating several times that life was fairly normal during the Occupation, there was an ever-present fear of what the Japanese might do to you. There were lots of stories about what had happened to people.

Then came the day when all the toy guns had to be registered. Apparently, there had been several incidents of Japanese soldiers being held up in the dark by Filipinos with toy guns. I had several cap pistols, including a small one called a Dick that I had gotten in a trade; the one I used to hold up the American outside the Admiral Hotel before the war, which is called an Army 45 and modeled on the real 45; and a beautiful Western revolver whose cylinder rotated when you fired a cap, and several others. I also had my Benjamin air rifle. After we registered them, I was able to take mine home.

We were getting hungrier and hungrier because there wasn't that much food available anymore, the air raids having played havoc with the food distribution system. Actually, unlike the United States, food was never rationed. You could always buy some

about it, opened the scratch, squeezed the pus out, and put some Mercurochrome on it. Didn't even bother to tell the folks since they would have done the same thing. Slowly but surely, the infection got worse. The Mercurochrome was three years old and may have lost its effectiveness, and with our constant hunger our natural resistance was pretty low. The sore got bigger and bigger and the lymph glands in my left

Troops patrolling on Padre Faura Street; buildings of the University of the Philippines.

provided you had money. Besides food, another scarcity developed, namely toilet paper. We all took to cutting up old newspapers into little squares. Neho said that Gaston had come up with an idea of making the squares last longer. One jammed one's finger through the square, used a finger to wipe one's self, and then wiped off the finger with the paper. That way, one could get by with only one square of paper instead of several. They both laughed when they explained it to me, so I assumed they were only kidding. I never tried that method, though I did use the squares.

In early January 1945, I had a small scratch on the middle knuckle of my left hand and it got slightly infected. I didn't think too much

armpit started to swell. A Belgian doctor, Dr. Hertz, had moved into the Egeas' servants quarters, having been evicted by the Japanese from his house, and he pushed a needle into the sore to see at what point I could feel it. I guess it was a way to measure the depth of the infection. Anyway, the needle went in up to half its length before I felt anything.

One of our neighbors wanted to put a green square piece of cactus on the sore to draw out the poison, but I wouldn't have any of that. With my swollen lymph glands they said that if things didn't improve in a day or two they might have to amputate my arm. Not knowing any better, I thought that would be an interesting experience and I would be unique. Finally, from somewhere, I believe it was from the Peters, they got two white pills that they crushed and put on the wound, and then things improved. I believe they were sulfa tablets. For a while, I had to keep the hand tied to a small board so that it would be immobile and I kept the arm in a sling. When the board was taken off, my hand looked really strange; the hairs on the back of it all stood straight up.

One afternoon, I was sitting in my room and thought I smelled Japanese. They frequently had a sweet pomade-like smell, possibly from pomade they put in their hair. I hadn't heard a thing, but when I looked out my window, I could see a whole column of soldiers walking along España Extension, which was a block away from us across some open fields. There were one or two small cannons being pulled by the soldiers. They were lucky there weren't any American planes around, though that late in the afternoon there usually weren't any.

Near the end of January, we stayed mostly close to home, though I still visited the Prieurs. Once we visited the Peters at their new home with the Gutierrezes and we played on top of their big, dirt-covered air raid shelter. Mr. Peter came to visit us after that and told us that some Japanese had shot at him. He ducked into a field of cassava plants, which grow quite tall, and managed to get to our house unhurt. After that, he didn't come to visit anymore until after the Liberation.

One hot noon, I looked out a window and saw a Japanese soldier with his helmet covered with leaves as he patrolled the street. Another time, during an air raid, I looked out and saw two of them taking shelter under some trees growing alongside a house across the street. I remember feeling pity for those guys having to be out in the hot sun with their steel helmets on, even if they were the enemy.

Around this time, a small Japanese panel truck overturned on España Extension, and Mr. Lienhard and I went to take a look. We could see some packages in the back of the truck because the rear doors had opened, and we hoped that it was food and that the soldier would offer us some. Instead, he waved us away, but then I guess he was in a bad mood and it may not have been food anyway. We knew from the daily paper that the Americans had landed in Lingayen and that it would only be a matter of time until they arrived. What a wonderful time that would be!

RODERICK HALL'S NARRATIVE

During the war Dad received a few letters through the Red Cross from grandmother in Edinburgh, Scotland, addressed to "Alaistair Cameron Hall, British Civilian Prisoner of War, Santo Tomas Internment Camp, Manila, Philippines." One letter said "Henry reports that Joe plans to spend his next birthday with his family." This passed the various censors. Those mentioned were my two uncles, Captain Henry McMicking an intelligence officer with the US Army Air Corps in England, and Lt. Colonel Joe Mc-Micking, with General MacArthur's staff in the Pacific. This gave an estimated date of March 23rd for the liberation of Manila, only three weeks after the battle finally ended.

Several months before the first air raids began, the Japanese requisitioned all houses fronting on Dewey Boulevard facing Manila Bay. The many coconut palms that made this boulevard so pretty were cut down and a landing strip for fighter planes constructed along the highway. The entire area became off limits, and we could no longer play there.

On September 21, 1944, a day engraved in our memory, Ian and I were sitting at a card table on one end of our porch, with our tutor Dr. Modry, when the sound of airplanes and explosions interrupted our lessons. The sky was full of strange single-engined airplanes. It only took us a minute to realize they were American, and probably from an aircraft carrier. We watched as they flew across and around, in dogfights with Japanese airplanes. There was a lot of anti-aircraft fire, and we could hear the shrapnel falling. We were so excited that we ran out to collect the shrapnel as soon as we saw a piece fall. The small sharp pieces of metal were red hot, silver colored and very shiny. Days later all rusted. It was quite a day for us, and everyone was excited, thinking the Americans would be back in Manila in a few short days. It took much longer, too late for many of my family. My sister Consuelo recalls watching Mom playing Mah Jong with our grandmother and aunt Helen, when a piece of shrapnel came through the window and embedded itself in the dining room table.

I don't recall seeing any Japanese planes flying after those first few days. Carrier planes returned many times, in groups of two or three, looking for targets of opportunity. We could hear anti-aircraft guns firing nearby, but could not see any guns. One day, on Padre Faura I think, we saw the burned-out chassis of ten Japanese trucks destroyed when hit by a fuel tank jettisoned by a carrier plane.

Once the air raids started many more Japanese soldiers could be seen in our neighborhood. They put up road blocks with barbed wire, manned by a sentry. When we approached a sentry we had to bow properly and say something in Japanese like "I live over there" and they would let us through. We stopped our school lessons.

On the morning of January 20, 1945, two weeks before the liberation of Santo Tomas Internment Camp, a tragic event occurred in our lives. We were sitting at home, on the porch. I was not wearing any shoes because of a fungus infection. As usual, my aunt's fiancé, Carlos Perez Rubio, was present. At about 10 a.m. there was loud pounding on our front gates; they flew open and a skirmish line of Japanese soldiers approached the house, carrying rifles with fixed bayonets. Yells and loud talking in the kitchen, were followed by the servants prodded by more troops with rifles and fixed bayonets. We were herded together in one end of the porch, and the soldiers began a three-hour meticulous search of the house and attic. All suspect items were collected. Many soldiers had been held up by Filipinos armed with nothing but toy pistols, so all had been ordered to turn such items in. Mom let Ian and I each keep one favorite pistol. These were found, as well as some radios, including a short wave radio Uncle Alfred used to listen to war news.

Maria Lopez Mena, the lady who had come to live with us after being evicted from her own home, was not present, but returned, and, insisting to the guards at the gate that she lived in the house, was let in. Fortunately, my youngest brother Allie and sister Consuelo were playing at a neighbor's, and were not present.

A list of everyone in the house was compiled. The men's arms were tied behind their backs and, surrounded on all sides by soldiers with fixed bayonets, we were marched 8 blocks to the Masonic Temple on Taft Avenue, Japanese Marine Headquarters. We were made to stand in the yard in the sun until grandmother asked if the women and children could sit in the shade. Water was offered, but no food. Also present in the yard, arrested that morning, were several other groups from the neighborhood.

In the late afternoon a Japanese soldier came out and started reading names from the list that had been compiled. He pointed and said "As I read your name, you will move over there". First they called Uncle Alfred and Carlos Perez Rubio, then Aunt Helen, my mother and grandmother. I was called next, and started to follow when the officer said "No, no, you go over there", pointing the other way. My group included brother Ian and all the servants. This procedure was repeated with the other groups. When all names had been read, and we had been segregated in two groups, the soldiers

marched us to the front gates and released us. We made our way home, expecting the rest to be released later. Our group included our Chinese amah Ah Nam, the housekeeper Maria Pena, and five Filipino servants whose names I do not remember.

Those taken from our home that day were:
Mrs Angelina Rico de McMicking, my grandmother
Mrs Consuelo McMicking Hall, my mother
Miss Helen McMicking, my aunt
Lieut. Alfred McMicking, my uncle, a survivor of the Bataan Death March
Miss Marita Lopez Mena, a family friend
Mr Carlos Perez Rubio, my aunt's fiancé

Following the arrest we were allowed to send meals daily to the Masonic Temple. We packed hot food in enamel containers that stacked on top of each other. About a week later we were told to stop sending

Photo taken on a garden bench at 740 Dakota Street, Malate, Manila about 1938 by my uncle Joe McMicking. First Row (left to right): Helen McMicking (killed by the Japanese in January, 1945); Ian Hall; Alaistair "Allie" Hall; and Roderick Hall. Second Row (left to right): Consuelo McMicking Hall (killed by the Japanese in January, 1945); Jose McMicking (died of a stroke on January 3, 1942) holding his granddaughter, Consuelo Hall; Angelina Rico McMicking (killed by the Japanese in January, 1945); Alaistair "Shorty" Hall; and Mercedes Zobel McMicking.

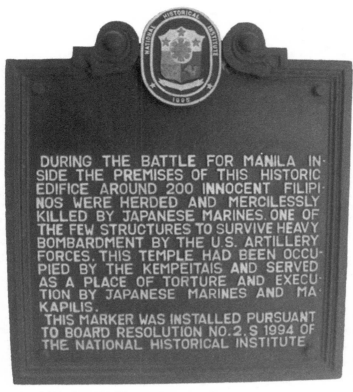

DURING THE BATTLE FOR MANILA IN-
SIDE THE PREMISES OF THIS HISTORIC
EDIFICE AROUND 200 INNOCENT FILIPI-
NOS WERE HERDED AND MERCILESSLY
KILLED BY JAPANESE MARINES. ONE OF
THE FEW STRUCTURES TO SURVIVE HEAVY
BOMBARDMENT BY THE U.S. ARTILLERY
FORCES. THIS TEMPLE HAD BEEN OCCU-
PIED BY THE KEMPEITAIS AND SERVED
AS A PLACE OF TORTURE AND EXECU-
TION BY JAPANESE MARINES AND MA-
KAPILIS.
THIS MARKER WAS INSTALLED PURSUANT
TO BOARD RESOLUTION NO. 2, S 1994 OF
THE NATIONAL HISTORICAL INSTITUTE

gates each night. I have always thought it ironic that while the family were held by Japanese Marines, we were protected by the Japanese Army.

It was at this time that I fell ill with amoebic dysentery. Our doctor prescribed medicine. Ian, who was in charge of our small amount of cash, arranged to buy it at the local drug store, near Malate Parish Church. We were charged 500 pesos in Japanese Occupation money, an exorbitant amount then; a few weeks later this money was worthless. The medicine cured me.

food. We thought this was because they had been transferred to Fort Santiago, but after the liberation it was discovered that our family members were among more than one hundred people executed at the Masonic Temple. They were identified from the charred bodies.

A few evenings after the arrests, there was a pounding at our back gates, and when opened, some bandits entered with guns and ransacked our house for things of value, such as automobile tires, rice, etc. They remained for the night and were collected by bus the next morning at 5 am. A Spanish friend of Mom's, married to a German national, complained to Japanese Army Headquarters, and for a few evenings we had sentries posted at the front and back

HANS HOEFLEIN'S NARRATIVE

On September 21, 1944, when the air raids started, Dad was at work and I remember him calling Mom on the telephone saying, "Don't worry about it, it's only a practice air raid", because the Japanese had announced the day before that they were going to have a huge practice air raid. My Mom said, "We'd better worry about it because a bomb just fell next door." So, Mom and I went into our neighbor's air raid shelter. They had built it above ground out of wood and then covered it with dirt. We went there whenever there was an air raid because we were near the bay and there was always a lot of shrapnel falling down from the anti-aircraft fire. The Japanese used a lot of 25mm automatic anti-aircraft ammo, which had an impact fuse, so if it didn't hit anything it would explode when it came back down and hit the ground. Besides injuring a lot of people from the shrapnel when they exploded in the air, they also caused a lot of fires after exploding on the ground.

Furthermore, American planes were making their bombing runs for the ships in the bay right over our house and if a plane got hit you never knew where it would crash. Right after an air raid, we would frequently hop on our bicycles and look for the crashed planes, both Japanese and American. We would go to Nielsen or Nichols fields, neither of which were that far away. At that crash site, we would see two types of crashes. If the pilot was able to make a belly landing in a field, the plane would still be pretty complete. If the pilot crashed into the ground, all you saw was a big hole with a lot of little bits of metal around it. We never ran into any Japanese at the crash sites, and my porch soon had lots of little pieces of crashed Japanese and American planes. No, we never saw any dead pilots. Either they had bailed out, managed to get out of their belly-landed aircraft, or had been blown to pieces if the plane went straight into the ground.

Most of the time, we went into the air raid shelter, but once in a while I would sneak out and, either go to my friend in the Michelle Apartments and watch from his floor as the planes attacked the ships in the bay, or I would go across to the Apostolic Delegation and watch from there. While we had a higher view from the apartments, the delegation was closer to the bay and one could see better from there. I saw a few ships get hit.

The part of Dewey Boulevard from the Yacht Club to Pasay had been converted by the Japanese into a take-off strip for Japanese planes. They had taken out the center section of the boulevard in that area and then built a ramp at the Yacht Club, so that they could land disassembled planes by barges from the bay, assemble them, and then take off. They were all single-engined planes, and my friends and I used to watch this activity from the Michelle Apartments. We also watched the Japanese soldiers train at Fort San Antonio Abad. They were rather ludicrous because they were training with bamboo poles, to which they would attach explosives to use against tanks.

At that time, I still had no fear of the soldiers and with the little Japanese I had learned at La Salle I was able to carry on some rudimentary conversations. It wasn't until the battle for Manila that I became frightened of the Japanese.

The Japanese used to print the Occupation currency in Japan and then bring it in by ship. During one raid, one of those ships got hit and soon it was raining paper money all over the streets. Everyone thought they were getting rich, but the Japanese refused to accept any of the notes, most of which had been burned or damaged in the explosion. I also remember that a lot of the smoke puffs from the Japanese anti-aircraft were of different colors, which was their way of determining range and distance. It wasn't that effective because there were not many American planes shot down.

HANS WALSER'S NARRATIVE

On September 21st, 1944, I was walking along Dewey Boulevard right next to Manila Bay. The Japanese were putting on an exhibition of their accuracy with anti-aircraft fire. Japanese airplanes were flying slowly through the skies over Manila Bay dragging targets behind them. Japanese guns were destroying these targets with great accuracy. I watched these goings-on with nonchalance. All of a sudden, there was airplane machine gun fire and a Japanese plane burst into flames and went down into the bay. More firing and another Japanese plane plunged into the bay. Now, this caught my interest; this was different. The air raid siren sounded. The anti-aircraft guns started firing more often. I watched as planes shot at other planes and witnessed my first dogfight. Some more Japanese planes went down. What was going on? It was then that I saw the insignia on the wings of an American plane. Then I saw it on more planes. Evidently, the planes had initially cut their motors and come into this exhibition without anyone detecting them. The people, mostly Filipinos, all cheered and jumped all over themselves with joy. All waved at the American planes, which I am sure were too busy with other things to notice. These cheering people were lucky they were not shot by the Japanese soldiers on the street. The Japanese soldiers were scurrying around looking for someplace that would provide protection. The anti-aircraft guns, that were very accurate hitting targets, really opened up, but I don't think they hit one single American plane. Of course, the planes were flying faster than the planes dragging targets and they weren't flying in a straight line. I will never forget that day. For me, for us, for all the Filipinos, all of a sudden, there was hope.

For the next several days American planes raided the area. There were dogfights and bombings of Japanese fortresses outside the city. The airfields were hit hard. It didn't take long for the Americans to establish air supremacy.

During the last couple of months in 1944, the Americans started a harassment air campaign. Every night around midnight one lone bomber would fly around the skies over Manila. The Japanese searchlights would try to find him and then the anti-aircraft guns would open up to try to shoot him down. The plane was never hit. When the searchlight would find the plane and focus on it, the pilot would dive down right at the light and the Japanese, fearful that he would drop a bomb on them, would shut the light off. After a while flying around and with all the noise from the guns keeping us awake, the pilot would decide that the amount of gas he had left was needed to get him home. Then he would dive down on some target and drop his bomb. Then he flew home. This happened night after night, keeping us all awake. Even the dogs knew what was going on (we still had a few dogs at that time that hadn't been eaten). Before anyone could hear the American plane coming, the dogs heard it. And they knew that a lot of noise would ensue so they started barking. Hence, before the plane got over Manila, we all knew from the dogs that it was coming.

I do not remember when my father stopped working. Obviously, there came a time during the Occupation that planes and ships could not come in or go out and there was no need for an import/export firm.

Life was starting to get less and less "normal". Often people were rounded up off the street and driven to the outskirts to work on dummy airfields. The Japanese reasoned that the Americans would use a lot of bombs on these air-strips. Japanese soldiers often yelled or hit passers-by.

Food was no longer in plentiful supply. Valentina needed to take more trips to the big Pasay market and to the small market we had a block and a half away. Markets were big open areas with a tin roof on top. Many vendors would bring their wares and set up benches to display them. Meat went from carabao and horse to dog to cat and some said to mouse. Prices started to climb. Currency was still that Japanese Occupation money and the vendors knew that would soon be worthless. We still had our little vegetable garden, banana tree and coconut tree, all in the front yard. My father thought we should have an alternate means of getting water, so we dug a well in the front yard. While we were able to get water, it was very muddy and certainly not desirable to drink. More and more of the young Filipino kids were walking around the neighborhood with bodies showing a lot of bone under their skin, but also with distended bellies, the sign of beri-beri.

After the invasion of Leyte, prices for food just soared. In January 1945 a sack of rice was P12,000, a sack of sugar P14,000, meat (any kind you could get) was P1,000 a kilo, eggs P60 each. Pechay had disappeared from the market and camotes went up to P300 a kilo. We were compelled to sell some of our household goods in order to buy some of the food or simply use these goods as barter. Fortunately, we had stocked up on sugar and rice. The big market in Pasay was still open but the small market near us had been confiscated by the Japanese for an airplane-engine repair shop. By the middle of January there was little interest in the Japanese Occupation money but you couldn't use the old Philippine peso. People caught doing so landed in Fort Santiago for punishment. In January you needed to exchange some tangible thing to get food since no one would accept the Japanese money.

By the end of January, my father, who used to be a kind of pot-bellied man, weighed 115 pounds and my mother weighed 85. And food was soon to become scarcer and then cease to exist for us.

At the beginning of January 1945 the Japanese Army moved out of Manila. General Wachi left too and the Chinese man returned to his house. The city was then taken over by so-called Japanese Marines, a wild looking crowd. Many had no shoes and not even guns. The Japanese were low on lead, so they manufactured wood and even cardboard bullets (I happen to have a couple). When the soldiers of the Japanese Army left the houses that they had taken over that were near us, Filipino looters moved right in and stripped the houses of everything. We could see them all day going along the street carrying the various articles from the houses, including a few of the houses on Fresno Street. Towards the middle of January, our lonely Leveriza street got to be a busy place. One Sunday morning when we woke up, we heard picks being used. Looking out the window, we saw a group of Japanese soldiers tearing up the street in front of the gate leading into the Case compound. When they found the ground too hard to make headway with their picks, they used dynamite. The blasts sent big rocks on top of the roof of our house. They made 3 tank-traps in our neighborhood one in front of Mrs. Case's gate, one at the corner of Leveriza and Balagtas and one at the corner of Leveriza and Fresno, all just yards away from our house. Between the tank-traps they planted at least 10 landmines and marked these mines with a few innocent looking stones. Whenever we left our house we had to remember to walk around all these mines and traps. But our ability to leave our house and go out onto Leveriza street was soon to come to an end.

CHAPTER VII

LIBERATION

JUERGEN GOLDHAGEN'S NARRATIVE

On the evening of Saturday, February 3, 1945, a small rescue column of the US First Cavalry Division entered Santo Tomas and liberated the internees, and started the battle for Manila and its Liberation. We in Quezon City did not know about this at the time it happened.

That same day, the Japanese told our neighborhood that we would have to leave our houses because the next day, Sunday the fourth, starting at 10:00 a.m., they were going to blow up the ammo dumps in front of our houses. We could go back home when the explosions stopped. Of course, we could stay in our houses, but it was extremely dangerous.

Fortunately for us, the pile that had been in front of our house had been removed by this time. There was still a large pile in front of the Carvajals' house, another one about three houses away from us, and then lots of other piles along various parts of Nevada Street, but not in front of any houses. There were going to be lots of explosions with shells and shrapnel flying around, so one had to find shelter somewhere. We went to the Prieurs' house, where they had a high adobe wall surrounding the house, no ammo dump nearby, and best of all they had a nice roomy cellar. Most houses in Manila do not have cellars.

We got there around 9:30 a.m. and Neho, Gaston, and I watched the explosions from

The Goldhagen home from 1944 to 1947.

the second floor of the garage annex. It was beautiful to see the arching smoke trails as dumps blew up at a distance, but as the explosions got closer, we joined the rest of our families in the cellar. And so, things banged and roared until around 3:00 p.m. Then we left the basement, and went out and looked down Nevada Street. We could see there was still an unexploded dump toward our house, so we decided to wait another half-hour. Though we had been told when the demolitions would start, no one had any idea when they would finish.

Finally, we decided that they weren't going to blow up the dump we saw and we walked home. There were shell fragments all over the road and many of the electric wires were hanging down from their poles. There were no sparks because there was no more electricity. I walked with great care in my wooden bakyas because I didn't want to slip out of them and step on a sharp shell fragment. Bakyas, which I wore a lot in those days, are a piece of wood shaped to the length of a foot, with a canvas strap across the front for you to slip your foot into. The strap could be made of canvas for cheapness and durability or of softer material for more comfort. The strap could also be stylish and colorful with beads for decoration. Being a hardy teenager, mine was made of plain canvas.

Fortunately, our home had only incurred some minor damage. We had a few tiles knocked down in the kitchen, and in my room several windows had been blown out. After the Liberation, we used cardboard from U.S. Army ration boxes to replace the glass windows. Besides, having no electricity, we also found out that the water had been cut off.

The Carvajals, having had a dump in front of their house, had more damage and even had an unexploded shell that landed in the window bars of their kitchen. A nice thing to look at and think about when doing the dishes, never knowing if it would explode at any time. The Americans finally took it away.

My room in Manila. We used cardboard from food boxes to cover the broken glass in the windows on the left hand side of the picture. The glass was broken by exploding Japanese ammunition.

The Egeas had beautiful green glass sliding doors that they had closed to keep out any looters. All the glass was blown out by the concussions. Luckily, there were no looters, but even they knew that they could get killed by the explosions and that they would be shot on sight.

Besides ammo, Mr. Lienhard told me that one of the boxes had had horseshoes in it. I never noticed them, but Mr. Lienhard, being an avid horseman, did.

At that time, we had a dog named Pursil and we had wanted to take her with us to the Prieurs, but we couldn't find her when we went. We thought she had been killed, but after two or three days she turned up. After that, whenever there was a thunderstorm, she would start to whine and crawl under the furniture.

The next morning, Monday the fifth, we heard a rumor that the Americans had liberated Santo Tomas on Saturday the third. Rumors were the only source of news because there was no more radio or newspaper. So, we figured that they must be at the Quezon Institute and we would be freed that afternoon or the next morning.

On one of those mornings, I was playing in the Egeas' backyard and had carved a futuristic auto design out of a small piece of adobe stone, when Mr. Egea walked past. He was accompanied by two Japanese officers who had grenades dangling from their belts. I had no fear for a change because they seemed friendly, but they were ready for combat. I had never seen any of them walking around wearing grenades before.

Then, one afternoon, I saw flames shooting up from under the roof of a local market hall a distance away. Things were being destroyed by the Japanese because they were going to be pulling out shortly. What would happen to us? Would we have to take to the fields with our rucksacks? I knew that we could easily hide in the fields around our house, never dreaming that we wouldn't be given any advance warning. The Japanese would have put a guard at the front and back doors of our house, and then come in and gotten us and shot us. Or they would have burned the house and stood watch outside, and shot us as we tried to flee. We later learned that that happened to a lot of people in the city.

Since we had no electricity, Mom had a small native clay cooking stove that could hold one pot on top of it. It was fueled by wood and we would gather whatever branches we could find to feed it. We got drinking water from a community well a few blocks away and then had to boil it first. We also took water from a nearby creek to use for flushing our toilets. Mr. Lienhard got hold of a large empty oil drum from the Japanese

and had taken the top off. We then put in a small amount of water and lit a fire under it to boil off some of the oily residue. This was going to be our container for catching rainwater.

On February 7, Wednesday, we heard a rumor around noon that the Americans were now in Kamuning, a nearby residential area, but by then we didn't believe it. There still wasn't any sign of the American Army and the Japanese were still around. About 3:00 p.m. that afternoon, we heard a plane flying very low overhead and, looking out of an upstairs window, I saw it was a small US Army observation plane, like a Piper Cub. We then heard machine gun fire from the machine gun unit across the street and thought they were shooting at the plane. With the gunfire, we didn't dare look out of any windows.

By 3:30 p.m., everything had quieted down and, looking out of an upstairs window, I saw a column of Japanese soldiers with helmets, rifles, and field packs walking on Nevada Street toward the intersection of Sta. Mesa and España Extension, away from our house. As they marched away, a small wooden shack at the corner of Nevada Street and New York Avenue, about half a block away from us, was burning. It most probably contained some supplies that they couldn't take with them.

About the same time, some Filipinos who lived across the street from us came and asked if they could take shelter in our house. They did this because they knew we were Germans and they knew that the Japanese wouldn't harm us. We invited them in and fortunately they were right but, as we later learned, being German was not a guarantee of anything in the city.

About 5:00 p.m., we heard some squeaky noise at a distance and I went upstairs to look out of Mr. Lienhard's window, but I couldn't see anything. Yet the noise persisted and then suddenly I saw an American tank across the fields. It was solid green, unlike the Japanese tanks, which always had camouflage painting, had a white star on the turret, and was just different from the Japanese tanks. It was moving on one of the dirt roads by the Green House where we had lived with our goats, and then it stopped and started firing a machine gun in its turret towards the house. I could see the smoke from the gun, which was near its cannon. It did not fire the cannon. I thought, it's hurting our old house and if I can see them shooting, they can also see me and I had better get away from the window before I get shot. I went downstairs and everyone was wondering where I was. I looked at a grandfather clock we were keeping for the Filipino family that had sought refuge with us and, I thought, I must remember this time and date because we have been freed! It was 5:30 p.m. on Wednesday, February 7, 1945.

A little later, Mom, Dad and I went to the upstairs porch and saw Mr. Lienhard approaching some American tanks in a field about two blocks from the back of our house. I wanted to run out and join him, but my folks wouldn't let me. Mr. Lienhard was lucky he wasn't shot either by any remaining Japanese or by the American tanks, mistaking him for an enemy.

To celebrate our liberation, I opened a can of Karo corn syrup from our precious supply of canned goods in the closet and started to have a tablespoon or two. It was a great luxury for me, but I was quickly satiated and did not finish the can.

Dad advised all of us in the compound to keep very quiet and to keep a low profile with no celebrating of any kind. For the next two days, everything was very quiet, we stayed in our houses in the compound, and no troops of either side were to be seen.

Some Filipinos nearby celebrated a bit prematurely, and Japanese stragglers killed them in the night and burned their houses. I saw one of the houses burning and yelled for my folks, who had gone next door to visit a neighbor, to come home.

Then on the second afternoon after we had seen the tanks, we saw some troops in green uniforms about two blocks away. They looked like Filipinos and we were all frightened that they might be Makapilis. The Makapilis were Filipinos who were loyal to the Japanese and had been armed by them. The Makapilis were considered low-class bullies who had sold out their country and were even meaner than the Japanese. The Carvajals thought the soldiers we saw were Filipinos in the US Army and started to wave and cheer. Fortunately, the Carvajals were right.

Later that afternoon, two or three Filipinos started across España Extension through the rice fields on the other side and up an incline to attack Dr. Moncado's residence. They were extremely brave and as I watched from upstairs they seemed to be pinned down by rifle fire from the doctor's house. Once they were pinned down, I got tired of watching and went downstairs.

Most probably, they were a diversionary tactic and the main attacking force was coming at the Japanese from the other side. There was no way these three men were going to capture the house, which had a wall surrounding it and was occupied by the Japanese.

Then, late on the afternoon of February 9 or 10, I was walking home from some nearby fields where Dad had moved the ammo dump that had been near our house. When we got home after all the ammo explosions had stopped, that dump near our house still had not been blown up. Dad talked to the Japanese and convinced them that he could get the Filipinos, who lived in the nipa hut that was right next to the dump, to move the ammo to an open field and there the Japanese could blow it up without harm to anyone. The Japanese agreed, and so Dad and the Filipinos moved the dump. Well, the Japanese did try to blow it up, but they did a sloppy job, with the result that there was small-arms ammo strewn all around the pile. Nice shiny ammo, ammo clips, and bandoliers. What a treasure trove for kids like me!

In other nearby fields were very large brass shell casings, also from partially blown ammo piles, which must have been for large artillery pieces. The shell casings were about four feet high and I was carrying one on each shoulder on my way home when I saw a patrol of American soldiers. They were walking by the corner of New York and Nevada Streets and, afraid that I might have something I shouldn't, I threw the shell casings into some bushes. I then ogled the soldiers and went past them into my house.

We invited one of them in and we wrote down his name and unit, but we lost it. We were sorry that we couldn't even offer him a drink of water because we had just boiled some water and it hadn't cooled off. He only stayed a few minutes because he had to rejoin his unit. One of the men had a radio pack on his back with an antenna and he was talking to an observer plane flying low overhead.

The next morning, which I guess was February 10, we saw truck after truck of GIs on España Extension going toward the junction at Santa Mesa Boulevard. By then, the Peters had come to stay with us, and Mr. Peter, Hans and I stood by the side of the road and cheered and cheered. The GIs would throw candy at us kids and packs of cigarettes at Mr. Peter.

Some of the three-quarter-ton trucks would slow to a crawl, and Hans and I would look in and see GIs sitting in them. We would reach in and shake their hands, and Hans kept saying "Victory Joe, victory Joe," but I was very quiet and shy. It was just so wonderful to know we were free again.

After about an hour of waving and getting Beeman's gum, Blackjack gum, Hershey bars, and cigarettes, we went home for a rest. Mom was in the backyard by the kitchen door cooking on the native, one-pot, wood-fueled stove and Mr. Peter asked her what kind of cigarette she would like, Camel, Chesterfield, Old Gold or Lucky Strike. Mom thought he was kidding and, when she realized he wasn't, she still couldn't believe it. Real American cigarettes after three years! As she told me years later, that was when she knew that the Americans had really returned.

Hans and I went back to the highway after lunch and stayed till about 3 o'clock. By then, there wasn't much traffic and we weren't getting any more goodies. One jeep even stopped and they said to us, "Are you two guys still here?" That convinced us to go home. It was such an emotional event. To this day, when I see scenes of the liberation in war movies or documentaries, my eyes always get teary.

Although we were liberated, the battle for the rest of Manila was going on in full force. Night after night, as we sat in our darkened house, lit by a candle or two, we could see flares in the distance and the glow of fires on the horizon. Mr. Mosert, one of our family friends, stopped me one night and said, "Stop and look at that, Juergen, for you will never see such a sight again". I stopped and counted the glow of seven fires on the horizon. Later, it came out that about 100,000 civilians died in the battle for Manila, and it is estimated that 60,000 died from Japanese atrocities and 40,000 from American shelling. The fighting went on until March 2.

RODERICK HALL'S NARRATIVE

The flying column of the First Cavalry Division entered North Manila and liberated Santo Tomas on the night of February 3, 1945, just 13 days after we had been arrested by the Japanese Marines. The Japanese military then pulled back from North Manila, to make their stand in the old Walled City and the districts South of the Pasig River. We remained at home until 15 February. It became dangerous to leave the house, as small bands of soldiers moved through the streets. At times they did not molest the few pedestrians, but they arrested people, and even entered houses, taking the residents.

Many near us were rounded up and taken to St Paul's Convent, two blocks away. It was the site of terrible atrocities on February 9, 1945. Survivors tell me they had been kept locked in the classrooms. That day the Japanese threw hand grenades into the rooms, causing many casualties. The explosions also tore through the walls, allowing the survivors to climb through and escape. As they ran, soldiers shot at them.

We heard the explosions from our home, and shortly after, waves of people came over our back wall, seeking refuge. All were worried the soldiers might follow, but they did not. We had over 150 people staying with us. As with most houses in our area, it was built about 5 feet off the ground because of flood risk. We all moved into this space to avoid the shelling that occurred sporadically throughout the day and night. The house never received a direct hit, but shrapnel rained down without warning. Shells landed on the lot next door, killing several people. Uncle Alfred had built a makeshift air-raid shelter under our house with sand-bags. We kept a corner, and shared the rest with the others. My sister Consuelo recalls the smell of the burlap sandbags and sleeping every night fully dressed.

Next door, the two-storey concrete home of the Brias Family had been commandeered for a headquarters. The soldiers moved out on the 6th or 7th of February, and that night we were thrown out of our beds by a terrific explosion. The house was completely destroyed. I woke with my eyes full of sand. Quite an explosion. The soldiers had built an air-raid shelter in the Brias' garden which was taken over and used by refugees.

Fires started everywhere around us, and swept through the mostly wooden houses, crossing the streets from block to block. Our large garden gave us some protection, but we worried our house might catch fire from the many large sparks. Our garage, adjoining the house next door, was destroyed by fire which did not jump to the house as the many men among the refugees kept a fire watch. I can remember one night when the fire risk was particularly bad, we all took our valuables out from under the house in case the roof caught fire. When the shelling started the rest of the family took shelter, but I stayed with the others as each protected their belongings from theft.

Most days, as shells whistled overhead, everyone would stand around outside until the whistling stopped, which meant that it was about to land and explode, at which point we would dive into the shelter. An Italian waiting too late was severely wounded in the buttocks. Since there were no anesthetics, that evening he was given a large dose of whiskey, held down by four men whilst the doctors among us tried to close his large wound. I held a kerosene lamp to provide light. He was delirious, and died later that night.

This brings up a fact no one considers. We lost all utilities: no electricity, gas, telephone nor water. Earlier in the Occupation Ian and I had dug a small well in the garden. The water table in our area was only 3 feet. With so many people, our water needs increased greatly, so the men dug our well deeper and rigged a pulley system. It had enough water for all, but needed boiling before drinking. The men also dug a well in the garden of the Brias' home. Charcoal was the main fuel used for cooking. We had kerosene lamps used sparingly for light at night, but no one stayed up very late.

Japanese patrols were all around our area, but none came into our garden. With our large hedge, they may not have been aware of the house. The people seeking refuge at home would stand or sit around all day, chatting to pass the time. They also prepared whatever food they had or could find, and I think there was a system for sharing, because most had lost all their possessions.

In the early afternoon of February 15th, one of the men sheltering at home called out "Hey, what are you doing here? You live in North Manila!" The other man replied "I've come with the Americans and they're half a block away. I'm looking for my family." "What, the Americans are here?" "Yes. Come along, I'll take you to them."

As the oldest member of the family, I went with three other men who had formed a committee. We crossed the street and, half a block away, sheltering under the intact galvanized roof of a burned out house, was an American GI. We sat and asked whether we should all move, or stay where we were. He replied "I am going to pull back tonight, but if you want to cross now, I'll help you

cross the lines." We returned to the house and after discussion, most decided to cross. I was told later that Japanese soldiers came into our house that night, but did not disturb the few who had remained.

There were snipers everywhere, as we carried a few belongings and walked in single file among the ruined houses, keeping well hidden. We could do so as almost every building in a 300 yard radius from our house had been destroyed by fire or shelling. Suddenly a sniper shot rang out and a little boy about 15 feet ahead of me fell. We all stopped to look at him as the GI yelled for us to take cover. We crossed through the middle of several blocks, and were joined by other GIs showing us the way.

After crossing several streets, we were held up because a Japanese machine gun controlled the next crossing. The GI with us ran half way across the street and dove the rest of the way before the machine gun could take aim, returning some half an hour later with a tank destroyer that parked in the middle of the intersection, and fired intermittently at the machine gun nest. We then crossed in small groups of two and three behind the shelter of the tank destroyer. Five blocks later the GIs told us we could remain there, safely behind the front lines.

That night, February 15th, we slept in the open. The night sky was lit up with tracers, flares and shell bursts, a tremendous display. Next morning an army jeep and trailer appeared with large containers of scrambled eggs, bread and coffee, to feed all of us refugees. We then started to make a shelter, clearing the tiled ground floor of a house that had burned. Suddenly I saw a relative, Arturo Ortigas, and said "Look at our new house." He replied "Oh my God, your father is frantic about you. Come on, I am going to take you to your father."

So our little group, Arturo, Ian, Allie, Consuelo, Ah Nam, Nena and I started walking through the rubble of the city. The only vehicles on the road were military. Heavy street fighting was taking place North of us, so we had to make a large detour to the East to get to Santo Tomas in North Manila to join Dad. Finally we got a ride in a GI weapons carrier, taking others to Santo Tomas, including a man who could not move his bandaged neck because his family had been beheaded by Japanese soldiers. He alone survived, his neck slashed deeply on the left, from back to front, but the artery had not been severed. A lucky survivor!

Arriving at the front gates of Santo Tomas, Dad was called, and we had a tearful reunion. He arranged for Ian and me to join him in the gymnasium with all the single men. Consuelo and Allie, who were younger, and Ah Nam and Nena Pena were given a room in the Seminary building where a

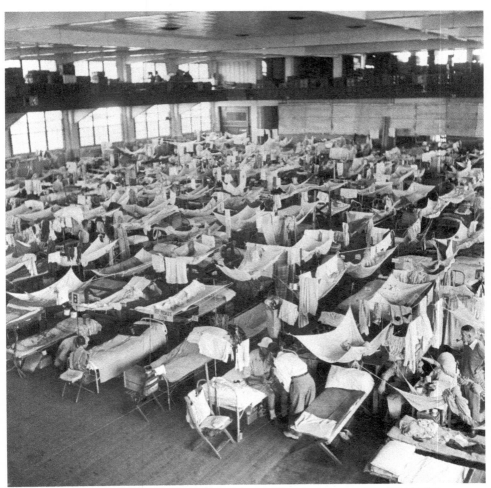

Crowded dormitory in the gym of Santo Tomas Internment Camp housing single men without families. Roderick and Ian Hall joined their father here after crossing the lines. (Photograph by Carl Mydans/Time & Life Books/Getty Images)

few University of Santo Tomas priests and nuns had remained when the University became an internment camp. Finally we were together with Dad and had been liberated!

HANS HOEFLEIN'S NARRATIVE

A few days before February 3, 1945, the Japanese kicked us and our neighbors out of our houses. They didn't provide us any means to move us and didn't tell us where to go, so we gathered a few belongings and we and a lot of other people went to the Remedios Hospital, which was about two blocks away. When we got there, there were already about 800 people on the hospital grounds, all thinking that because of the Red Cross markings on the roof and the fact that it was a hospital, they would be safe.

We had each carried a bag with tins of food and my mother had all our birth certificates and passports, which became essential later. It turned out that after we had all left our houses, the Japanese burned them and so everything we left behind was destroyed. We were lucky that they didn't force us to stay inside the houses when they burned them, as they did in many other sections of the city. They also set houses on fire and, as the people ran out, they shot or bayoneted them.

Fortunately, the tinned food we had brought lasted us for the time we were at Remedios, and water was available. About the same time that the Americans took Santo Tomas on the third, they had also taken the water reservoirs in the hills at Novaliches. This supplied water for the city of Manila and was a gravity-fed system, so when the Japanese destroyed the electrical system, the water supply was not affected, no pumps being necessary.

At first, things were fairly calm at the hospital, but then the shelling started and numerous shells fell into the hospital. The Japanese had started to shell Santo Tomas with guns placed a few blocks from the hospital, and the Americans shelled back. More and more people were getting killed on the ground by the shelling, including one of my best friends, Jaime Ventura. He, his mother, sister and aunt were all sitting near each other by a wall when a shell hit the wall; the wall collapsed and killed them. At this time there were bodies all over Remedios Hospital, including those of Jaime, his sister, parents and aunt. No one was there to remove the bodies and the stench was horrific. Pools of black coagulated blood and bloody rags showed where someone had been hit by shrapnel.

Then, one day the Japanese allowed anyone who wanted to go out on the street to do so, and soon there were about 200-300 of us sitting on the street with armed Japanese all around us. Luckily, they didn't do anything to us. Finally, my Dad and Mr. Fried decided to dig a hole big enough to shelter us all. Mr. Fried and his wife were a young couple who had recently married, and having been kicked out of their house before we were kicked out of ours, had moved in with us about two weeks before we were all kicked out.

So, Mr. Fried, Dad and I dug a large hole and then took the iron bars that used to be over the windows of some nearby burned houses, and put these bars across the top of the hole. Then, we took the galvanized tin roofs from some of those burned houses, and put them over the bars and piled dirt on top of that. So, we had a dugout that would protect us from all except a direct hit.

The night before we finished our shelter, poor Mr. Fried was hit by a piece of shrapnel that ripped his side open. Unable to endure the severe pain and thinking he was going to bleed to death slowly and in agony, he used some razor blades and slashed his wrists and quickly died. The next day, we finished the hole and then stayed in it for about two days. At night, we went out and got water and also did our bathroom requirements, though there was only the sides of the street to do those in.

We had opened a can of sardines, but my mother told us to eat sparingly of them because they would make us very thirsty. While in that hole, we had all come to the realization that we were going to die. Either from the shell-fire or Japanese atrocities, we knew we were going to die. Especially after listening to Mr. Fried die and the torments of his young bride. Once we reached that point, we didn't worry too much because there was no more point to it. We resigned ourselves to our fate.

Finally, on the morning of the February 16, still in our shelter, we heard a lot of people running around saying, "The Americans are here, the Americans are here!" We were very concerned because there were a lot of Makapilis around and we also knew by then that the Japanese were killing people.

So, we thought the Filipinos who were doing the shouting were Makapilis, who were trying to get people out of hiding so the Japanese could kill them. This went on for a while, and finally my mother peeked out of the shelter and saw some soldiers about 200 feet from us. She didn't recognize them as Americans because they didn't have on the World War I-type helmets they used in 1941. The helmets looked more like the Japanese type. Then, one of the soldiers gestured to her to come out and she gestured back to him, indicating she didn't want to. So, he took his helmet off and when she saw that he was blond she knew he was an American.

We then left the shelter, crossed the street to where the Americans were, and then were told to go to Welfareville, which was a building near the Paco railroad station that used to house orphans before the war. On the way there, we walked past lots of destroyed buildings and houses and a lot of dead Filipino civilians and Japanese soldiers. I took a steel helmet from one of the dead Japanese and it had a pack of cigarettes in it and a lot of blood. We spent the night there and the following day we crossed the Pasig River. Luckily, we found some friends there who had a house, and we rented a big room with a kitchen and we shared their bathroom. Most of the houses around the area had been destroyed and you found space where you could.

HANS WALSER'S NARRATIVE

Before I start in on the days of February 1945, I need to describe the layout of our house and the houses next to us as this will be very important as I describe the events that occurred that month. I want the reader to understand the very closeness of events. As I relate occurrences during February, they are happening just feet and yards away. I would like to take you to the site. Our house was two stories, a two-family house. We lived upstairs (the more desirable floor since we avoided the flooding during the rainy season) and occasionally, someone lived downstairs. During the 3¼ years of occupation, there were several times that the downstairs was occupied by another family. There were stairs on the left (looking from the street) front side leading to the upstairs and outside stairs on the left back of the house. The lot was a small lot. The lots were about the same size as the lot I live on now. A typical urban/suburban lot. However, there was a difference from the lot I live on today. All the houses in our neighborhood had concrete walls about 6 to 6½ feet tall in the front and the two sides. These side walls are important for one to conceptualize as you could not see what was happening in the next yard and anyone in the next yard could not see you. Likewise, the only way to see the street, or for people on the street to see you, was through the front gate. So events occurring a few yards away could be blocked from your view and you didn't know what was going on. But you could see into the next yard and the street if you were on the second floor of the house. These walls also were an encumbrance for one to get into the next yard. A large wall about 10 feet tall was in the back of our yard. In the middle of the front wall was an iron-grill gate that could be open and shut. Between the front of our house and the front wall were several yards of dirt which housed our garden and a couple of fruit trees. Behind our house were several feet of concrete and then the servants' quarters and garage. That was one structure with the garage on the right (if looking from the street), then the servants' space of small living room and 2 bedrooms, then a small area for an enclosed shower and toilet, and behind the shower a small dirt area (this is were I had my chickens). Behind the servants' quarters were about two feet of gravel and then that large wall. The driveway went from the center of the front where the gate was, angled around to the right side of the house and then into the garage behind the house. All the houses in the area had a similar construction with a front wall and gate and side walls for privacy. Our house and most of those around it were made of wood. Other houses in the neighborhood were partially made of concrete. The house (owned by a Chinese whose name I can't remember) on the right of us (looking from the street),

where the Japanese general had lived, was a big concrete house with a bigger, deeper front yard, a big house and a big back yard. The gate and driveway were on the left side of the house (again as looking from the street), next to the wall that separated us. The yard in front on the right had an air-raid shelter about 10 feet from the front wall and street. Looking from the street, our block of houses on Leveriza Street consisted of the Gonzales house to the left of us and on the corner of Leveriza and Menlo, our house, the Chinese person's house to the right of us, and another house to the right of that rented by Claro Recto. Then Fresno Street that went from Leveriza Street to Donada Street where the American School was. Opposite Fresno Street on the other side of Leveriza Street was a big open area with a well with good water. Menlo Street was on the other side of the Gonzales house and on Menlo Street, next to the Gonzales', was the Paris' house. Across Leveriza Street from us and the Gonzales house (and to the West towards Manila Bay) was the Case Compound of several houses; across from the Chinese neighbor's house were the Whitneys; and across from the Recto house were the Filers. Next to the Case Compound and North were the Balagtas Apartments, which were full of Japanese soldiers. A long block away (but still only one block) from us and to the North was Vito Cruz street and on the south side of that street, towards us, was the Perez-Rubio Compound. Across the street from the compound to the north were the Rizal Memorial Stadiums, the second largest Japanese defense area in Manila, where many Japanese made their last stand. The corner houses around Taft Avenue and Vito Cruz were fortified with pillboxes and machine gun nests. From our living space on the second floor, you could see into Leveriza Street, the houses next door and across the street, except for the area of the street right next to the front wall. Standing on the ground, you can't see the other yards because of the walls and you can't see the street except where the iron gate was. People on the street can't see you if you are in the back yard behind the house and they can only see into the yard if they look in through the gate.

The second theme I would like to emphasize is, how do you prepare for a big problem that is coming. We couldn't escape it, for we had nowhere to go. No relatives. Didn't think we could go South or North or East. Just to the West of us was Manila Bay. And how would we take anything with us? We had no car and not even a cart to push. So we had to stay where we were. Now what do you need—food, water, shelter, utilities, clothes, medicines and heat. And for us, most importantly, passports and papers. We had our shelter, our house; we had clothes on and in bureaus; we had running water and just in case, we put some water in our tub; we had food in the refrigerator, raw fruit and quite a few canned goods; we

had very little remaining of any medicine and that was in the cabinet; we didn't need any heat because it was hot out. But how much food and water would we need? We had no way of guessing and besides, it was too late to do anything about it.

On the night of February 3rd, we noticed fires way off in the downtown district of Manila. The Japanese had started to burn Manila. Early on Sunday morning February 4th, the Japanese posted a sentry at the corner of Leveriza and Menlo, a few yards away from our house. My mother and Valentina had just come home from the Pasay market and arrived just before the posting of the sentry. A few hours later we heard some explosions in the distance and immediately after that our lights went out, the refrigerator stopped working and we could no longer use the stove. Our electricity was gone. The water flow also stopped. We figured that the Japanese had blown up the Manila Electric plant and some of the bridges

What was left of the Legislative Building in 1945

that were used to pipe water throughout the city. We always expected that the Japanese would blow up the bridges and we knew that our water came through huge pipes over the Ayala bridge. For that reason we had tried to dig our own well. The only source of clean water was now the well in the empty lot across Leveriza Street at the corner of Fresno. For a few days afterwards we were able to haul water from that well to our house, but then the sentry at the corner of Leveriza and Menlo started to shoot at anything that moved. It happened just as the Chinese neighbor was on his way to get water. He was hit in the leg but managed to get back into his yard. That now took our water source away. At about noon on the 4th, Mr. Gonzales called my father over to the wall and told him that he had just heard that the American troops had occupied the internment camp Santo Tomas and Malacañan. My father told him it couldn't be true because he had heard on his short wave radio the night before that the Americans were still 30 miles away. But as we learned later, it was true.

Amazingly, during these first few days some parts of life tried to stay normal. On Sunday, February 4th, *The Tribune* still published its newspaper. Ana Ag Tabuena was married to Mariano Katipunan, Jr at the Santa Ana Church on January 31st. A concert musical jointly sponsored by the United Church Vested Choir and the Young People's Fellowship would be held at the United Church that afternoon at 3:30 with Professor Antonio Molina as guest speaker. New generals were being assigned to the Eastern Army District, the Tokai Army District, the Central Army District and the Western Army District. On January 29th, in the north, Japanese forces had attacked American positions and destroyed all their mortars. The Jai-Alai match would continue at 2:00 o'clock tomorrow. Members of the Aranga Badminton Club were busy getting in shape for their match with the Sabastian players.

So, with the sentry now being posted one house down from us, from now on, we couldn't leave our house and go anywhere on Leveriza Street and we made sure that we didn't go outside where we could be seen from the road. We kept away from the windows of the house as well. For the next few days we tried to keep track of what was going on by peeping above the lower window sill. Japanese soldiers went back and forth on Leveriza camouflaged; some even had small branches on their helmets. The water in the tub was quickly gone. Now for water, we had to have someone peek out of the front second floor window; determine that the coast was clear; have someone else sneak out the front door; go a few yards to our muddy well; scoop out some water; and run back into the front door. All the while we hoped no soldiers went by the front gate and hopefully we didn't make any noise to attract some. After all Leveriza Street was just several yards away from our front door. For food, we survived by opening some of the canned goods we had.

Meanwhile the fires from the north kept coming closer and closer. We hardly slept at all. During the days the sky was red from all the burning. On the morning of the 6th, around 4 a.m. we heard a commotion across the street at the Case compound. Peering out our window, we saw the Case house on fire, as well as the house next to it in the compound. The Japanese accused the Cases of harboring spies or guerillas. No one was allowed to take anything out of the houses. One of the tenants tried to rush out with a suitcase but a Japanese soldier stopped him, grabbed the suitcase and threw it back into the fire. While this was going on the other tenants were valiantly trying to move all their belongings out into the yard. From our second floor window, we could see the people running about from the flare of the fires. Mrs. Case, her daughter Ethel and the Walfords were taken for questioning to the Rizal Stadiums. The next day the Cases came back but the Walfords were never seen again.

On Thursday the 8th, an American plane flew low over our neighborhood and dropped leaflets. We were able to get one, and this confirmed that Santo Tomas and Malacañan Palace had been liberated. The fires in Manila to the north still kept coming closer and closer and we could estimate that they were now in the Ermita district. That evening fires started in the southern part of Manila as well. The Japanese were burning from the Pasay market.

On the morning of the 10th, while we were eating "breakfast", an American shell hit our house and exploded: the first American artillery shell in our area, and it had to hit our house. No one was hit but we all ran downstairs and into the downstairs kitchen. For some time shells were hitting our yard and all around us. Explosions were deafening and we got adept at figuring where the shell was going to land from the whistle while it was in the air. We figured that the Americans were trying to hit the Stadiums but didn't have the range. When the shelling quieted down, we went upstairs to see what the damage was. The floor was littered with glass and splinters of wood. And there were many holes in the northern wall facing toward Menlo Street. Then the shelling picked up again and it got so intense that we figured that since we had no real shelter of our own, we would use the air-raid shelter in our Chinese neighbor's front yard that had been built for the Japanese general. We had to get 2 boxes for each side of the wall to stand on in order to get up and over. I was a kid and fairly small. So, we would look out the second floor window, check to see no Japanese were coming, signal down for someone to climb over the wall, step on the boxes, go over the wall with what we were carrying and run to the shelter. We had to do this very quietly since we did not want the Japanese to hear us.

And the Japanese *were* all around us—we just didn't know where. (Listening for Japanese soldiers, running to the wall, stepping on the boxes, peeking over the wall to see if Japanese soldiers had entered the yard we were going into, going over the wall, and running for cover in the next yard, became a routine we did many, many times in the next few days.) If we had ever been spotted, we would have been killed. This for a 48-year-old man, a 45-year-old woman, a 22-year-old girl and me, almost 12 years old. Since the air-raid shelter was no more than 10 feet from the front wall and the street, and the Japanese soldiers occasionally walked up and down the street, we had to keep very quiet while in the shelter. In the afternoon of that Saturday, February 10th, in between the American artillery barrages, we moved our suitcases that we had packed with our papers, food and what we thought were necessities from our house to the shelter (each time going through the procedure of "lookout, climb, run"). Every now and then, we went back to the house to get a few things. A couple of the trips entailed getting our mattresses and mosquito nets. It was hard work and we were all sweating. By standing on the air-raid shelter, we could look out and see the neighborhood houses. During one such look, we saw the little market across the way beyond the empty lot, was in flames as were the houses around it. By 8 p.m. the shelling got too intense, we had to remain in the shelter. Other people in the neighborhood knew of that air-raid shelter and so by that night we had 11 people crouched in the shelter. When it was packed like that, no one could move. All night shells were hitting our area and the Stadiums. When they hit the Stadiums, we still would get debris and shrapnel from that hit. During a small, calm moment, my father went out of the shelter and told us that the Filers' house was on fire. This was right across the street from us; only a few yards away from our shelter. A little later we noticed fires at houses on Fresno Street only about 100 yards away.

Quezon Bridge over the Pasig River.

We learned the next day that the Japanese were now killing everybody they saw. They would go to a house, put one soldier at the front entrance and one at the back entrance, throw in incendiaries to make the house burn and shoot anyone who ran out of the burning house. So we knew the Japanese that night had been only a few yards away from where we were hidden. We also found out that when the Japanese came upon a group of civilians in an air-raid shelter, they just fired into the shelter or threw incendiaries into the shelter and shot you when you came out. Likewise for the houses in the neighborhood that were made of concrete. Toss in incendiaries and then shoot you when you came out.

The mosquitoes were very bad that night so you were bitten often when you left the protection of the mosquito nets. You couldn't slap at them since you couldn't make the slightest noise. During a lull (by lull I mean there sporadic gunfire and sporadic artillery, rather than constant), my father ventured out again but then red tracer bullets from the little market came towards him and struck only a few yards away, so he headed back to the shelter. During another lull I snuck up onto the top of the air-raid shelter and peeked out over the front wall. I saw red tracer bullets from the market hitting the area where the Filer house had been as well as the Whitney house. The Japanese in the Whitney house were firing back at the market. Mind you, this is going on right across the street, yards away from me. While watching, suddenly my subconscious took over and warned me that the whistle of an artillery shell indicated that the shell was going to hit near me. I quickly jumped down from the top of the shelter and dived into the shelter. Sure enough the shell landed in the front yard by the wall to our house, only yards from the air-raid shelter. The shock wave and shrapnel hit our shelter.

There was a lot of noise that night from the artillery shells, the machine guns and the rifles, as both American and Japanese soldiers fought house to house in our neighborhood. At about 5 a.m. on Sunday the 11th, my father made a mad dash to our house to get some food. In front of our house was an unexploded shell. He worried about what I would do if I came across it, so he picked it up and carried it out further into the yard. While carrying it, he did notice the US markings on the shell. Getting into our house, he noticed that it had been hit several times that night. He grabbed another box of food, and while carrying the food toward the side wall, noticed that part of our front wall by the street had been blasted out by a shell. It was not daylight yet, but just as he got to the side wall to climb over it, a bunch of Japanese soldiers in single file passed down the street by the front wall on the way to the little market. There were about 30 of them. My father froze but he never could understand how they did not notice him since they were only a few yards away. If they had, he would have been shot and all of us might have been discovered.

Around 7 a.m. there was another lull and we went over to our house to get some kitchen utensils and to bring back some cans of food to eat. A mestizo boy came over the southern wall from the direction of Fresno Street and reported that Mr. Stamm, a young Swiss, with whom he was living on Fresno Street, had been bayoneted at about 8 p.m. the previous night. The boy had escaped by diving through the window and hiding in the bushes next door. He then dashed across Leveriza Street and went into the Case Compound. The Japanese, after killing Mr. Stamm, then set the house on fire. (About a week later my father was sifting through that area and found only a few bones and his gold teeth in the ashes.)

Less than an hour later, a lavandera came climbing over the wall from Fresno Street and she reported having seen American soldiers at the little market. She also reported that 4 Spaniards had been killed by the Japanese the night before in a little compound where Dr. Eulau used to live, about 300 yards away. It turned out later that 2 of them were Mr. Dalan and his son. While she talked to us, we noticed fires towards the American School. The fires started spreading down Menlo Street towards our house. Then a housegirl came over the northern wall from Menlo Street and told us under tears, that the Japanese had killed all the people around Pax Court the night before. This is where Juergen lived for a while, and a few houses away from us. With all the shelling and gunfire around us, gunfire at Pax Court didn't catch any unusual attention from us. She also told us that the whole Perez/ Rubio family on Vito Cruz opposite the Stadiums and a block away to the North were massacred as well as their servants and the neighbors who had found refuge in their house. There were a total of 26 people killed. She had come from the side of the northern wall and was heading south. The previous visitors had come over the southern wall, going north. Everyone was in panic.

So within a block of our neighborhood, lots of our neighbors had been killed and houses were burning or had been burnt to the South, the West, the East and now the North of us. The Stadiums, where a strong force of Japanese were holed up, was still to the North of us, a block and a half away. We were still in Japanese territory with many Japanese soldiers in the streets and in many of the neighbors' yards around us. We just didn't know which ones. And we prayed they wouldn't look in or come though the gate or over the wall and into the yard where we were. At this time the American soldiers were a block and a half away to the South.

By now my father decided that staying quietly in an air-raid shelter about 10 feet

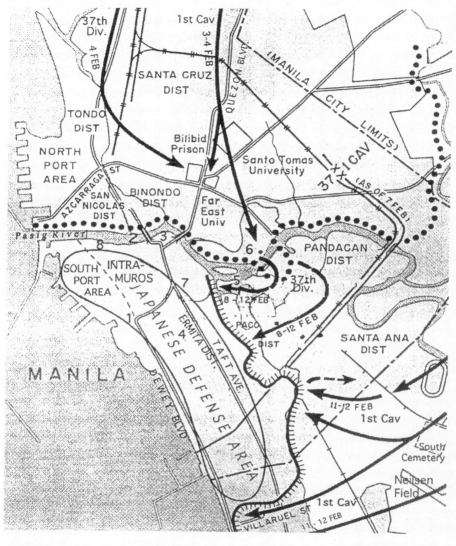

MAP 6 -- THE BATTLE OF MANILA

➤ U.S. AXIS OF ADVANCE, DATES INDICATED

●●●●●●●● U.S. FRONT LINE, EVENING, 7 FEB

ⅢⅢⅢⅢⅢ U.S. FRONT LINE, EVENING, 12 FEB

1 MANILA HOTEL
2 JONES BRIDGE
3 GENERAL POST OFFICE
4 EPISCOPAL CATHEDRAL
5 PROVISOR ISLAND
6 MALACAÑANG PALACE
7 LEGISLATIVE BLDG
8. FORT SANTIAGO

SOURCE: based on Robert
Ross Smith *"Triumph in
the Philippines"* Dep't of
the Army (1961), Map VI

SCALE MILES
       KMS.

108

away from the wall that bordered the street was an unsafe place to be. Staying in our unburnt house was also unsafe since the Japanese soldiers were burning the houses and shooting people coming out. So over the wall back to our house and over other walls he went to find a safer place. In climbing over to other yards we met the Paris family and the Gonzales family in their garages behind their houses. They already knew about the killings in the neighborhood. They invited our family to come over and hide with them and couldn't believe that we were holed up in a place so close to the street while Japanese soldiers were going back and forth. So my father took them up on their offer. It took us a very long time to make the move. We had to make several trips lugging our stuff over 2 walls. Again the routine. Be on the lookout for soldiers creeping up and down the street, then run to the wall with whatever you could carry, stand on the boxes, peer cautiously over the wall to see if any Japanese soldiers were in the next yard, quietly get yourself and the stuff you were carrying over the wall, run across the back yard, and then the same procedure for the next wall. And very, very quietly. While there was still a lot of American shelling going on, they now had the range of the Stadiums. So while the shells were going over us, we were still getting peppered by the shrapnel and concrete chunks from the Stadiums and an occasional shell that didn't have the range. Gunfire was still going on from the Japanese soldiers in our vicinity and from the American soldiers now about a block to a block and a half away. The noise from the shelling and the gunfire was loud enough to drown out any noise we made while moving. You just had to be very quiet when there were lulls in the firing.

While we were next door in the Gonzales' yard, a fire broke out at the Paris house, the next house on the other side. Mr. Paris brought one of his sisters over the wall into where we were. She had a shrapnel splinter in her leg and was in a great deal of pain. A couple of days ago, the Paris family and servants had moved a lot of belongings outside of the house and into the back yard. While their house was burning, Mr. Paris asked us to help save his garage where they were. He said he had a truck there full of gasoline that had been sitting there throughout the war. Their garage was near to the servants' quarters and garage of our house so if it caught fire, our house might go too. So again with a quiet procedure and over a wall, a bunch of us got water and succeeded in saving his garage, though his house burned down. Our house and the Gonzales house were temporarily saved. The Gonzales house was now the only house still standing on Menlo Street between Donada and Leveriza.

Just when we started to relax a little, the American shelling started up again and a shell hit the wall in the Paris yard. Fortunately, no one was hit. After it got quieter, we carried the Paris girl back into their yard and over two more walls into the garage in back of one of the houses on Menlo Street that was still burning. However, enough of the house remained upright so that you couldn't be seen from the road. We then decided that this probably was a good place to hide and so we went back and went through the whole procedure again of getting all our stuff over 3 more walls. It was not hard to figure out that the corner house and our house which were both still standing, were not the places to be. We didn't finish moving our stuff until the end of the day since there were many times we had to stop and hide. Shells were still hitting around us and the Japanese soldiers were still moving up and down the streets.

I should also point out that during the morning of that day, the 11th, we took a couple of our trunks and trunks of other people in Santo Tomas (trunks of the Loucks and others, since they could only take a few things into the internment camp) downstairs and into the yard, again always being on the lookout for soldiers. But in the afternoon it started to rain and when we got the Paris fire under control, we moved the trunks back into the ground floor of the house to get them out of the rain. In the middle of the afternoon, we saw that the remaining 3 houses in the Case Compound across the street were on fire. This while still moving our stuff over the 3 walls. So we now knew the Japanese had been or were directly across the street. On one trip my father was passing the servants' quarters in our yard when he felt a terrific air pressure suddenly and a loud explosion. An American shell had hit the servants' quarters and the blast took the roof completely off. So everyone ran back to our Chinese neighbor's air-raid shelter and we stayed there for a while till the shelling abated. We then continued moving our belongings to our new location and completed our moving just before darkness. We did not have an ideal location in that yard since other people had come before us and taken the more protected spots. We spread out our mattresses on the floor in the open garage and got our mosquito nets up. Nevertheless, we had a hectic night and when the shelling got quite heavy we had to move into an air-raid shelter in Paris yard since the tin roof on the garage where we were living was not very safe from artillery fire. February 11th was a very busy and hectic day.

On the morning of the 12th, a servant came over the wall, bringing news that a shell hitting Mr. Sabateur's house on Fresno Road had killed his daughter and two servants. This was about 100 yards from where we had been crouching in an air-raid shelter. He also told us that a family in a house on our side of Fresno Street had been shot by the Japanese and their baby had been tossed in the air and caught on a bayonet. Mr. Case across the street was also killed by shrapnel. Early in the morning we noticed smoke coming out of the Balagtas Apartments.

Fires were raging along the block between Donada Street and Taft Avenue to the East of us. Towards the South were additional fires along Taft Avenue in the direction of Pasay. The corner house on Fresno Street and Donada started to burn and we figured the Japanese would now burn the other houses on our side of Fresno Street; the houses on the South side had already all burnt down last night. (It turned out that none of them burned down since those houses had been made of concrete.) During that morning Valentina made several trips over walls to our house to get any food she could find and kitchen utensils so that we could open the cans of food and if practicable, might be able to heat something. During the morning the shelling increased but the shells were hitting the Stadiums and the Balagtas Apartments where a many Japanese soldiers were holed up. We still had shrapnel hitting us from the shelling and 2 servant girls who were trying to cook something got slightly hit a little after midday.

At 3:30 we saw the Gonzales' house, just two houses away from where we were (and the house right next to ours) go up in flames. So now we knew the Japanese were just 2 houses from where we were hiding. A few minutes later our house started to burn. The fire at our house was very intense due to the incendiaries being tossed in. While the house was burning, we heard a loud explosion as the dud shell that my father had moved further into the yard, exploded. We were now very sorry that we had moved the trunks back into the house when it had started to rain the day before. However, the trunks, even being outside, might not have survived the intense heat. There went all our belongings except what we had been carrying. No more shelter, no more of the little food that was in the house, no more clothes other than what we were wearing. If we had been in our house or in the yard at the time, we would have been killed. Gunfire continues all around us as Japanese and

American soldiers fought yard to yard and house to house in our neighborhood. The Americans were fighting their way towards the Stadiums.

About half an hour later we heard a commotion behind us and 2 Japanese soldiers came climbing over the South wall. Not good! Not good at all!! They lined up the people there and motioned all the people in the air-raid shelter to also join the line-up. I was the last one out. I came out carrying the steel cash box my father had. After all, my parents over and over again said to make sure we had that and not let it out of our sight. The box was very conspicuous when we were all made to raise our arms up. My father got very scared, for the box contained a few Philippine pesos, a few American dollars and our passports (including my mother's American passport). Everything we were not supposed to have. Both of the soldiers were pretty wild looking and kept yelling at one or the other of us lined up, and jabbing the bayonets on their guns at us. Then they talked to each other and we knew they were trying to decide what to do with us. Finally, after several minutes of ranting to one another, they just left us and went over the wall. It was a miracle that they didn't kill us. After all, some of us were white. My father thinks that they didn't start shooting us since there were far more of us than them. My father then took the contents of the steel cash box and put them into the bottom of a cracker can that contained sugar. About ten minutes later the two Japanese soldiers came back over the south wall. This time they didn't even look at us but went through a shell hole in the east wall, and into the next yard where the house was still burning.

Less than half an hour later, a Filipino with a gun appeared at the other side of the wall. He asked us whether there were any Japanese around. He also mentioned that an American patrol was just behind him.

We were very suspicious of him and didn't know whether to believe him or not since the Japanese soldiers had just left, but we told him that two Japanese soldiers had just left us and went into the next yard, that there were many Japanese soldiers in the Balagtas Apartments half a block away and a huge number at the Stadiums, a block away. He left us and about five minutes later showed up again with 6 soldiers. When we first saw the soldiers, we did not think they were Americans. They were very tan. In Manila, the Caucasians tried very hard to stay white and we just assumed that the American soldiers we would see would be white. It took us about a minute to really believe they were American. We stared at their faces (all we could see since they were on the other side of the wall) and they stared at us (some of us were white). It wasn't until one of them spoke that we fully accepted that they were American soldiers. Then some of our group just sat down and cried. The soldiers cautiously came over the wall and asked us how far away the Japanese were. We gave them all the information we had including the fact that 2 Japanese had just gone next door to the West. They asked us if we knew where mines had been planted and we drew a map of what we knew in the dirt. While doing this, rifle fire started to hit around us and we now knew a Japanese soldier had been watching us. The group hardly took notice. We moved just a few yards further west and further behind the burnt down house. One soldier calmly got up and headed north towards where the Japanese soldier must have been. We continued drawing the map and while doing so, heard a shot and a body came crashing down from a tree across the street. The American soldier then returned. Today, I can't comprehend how calm we all were during that episode and how nonchalantly we got up after the Japanese bullets hit near us, and just moved over a little bit.

A few minutes later they left us and moved

north across Menlo Street towards the Stadiums into the Roces compound, directly across from where we were. A few minutes later we could hear their guns firing and Japanese guns firing back. A half hour later one American soldier came back and told us he was going back to his unit to report what they had seen and heard. His American unit was stationed at the little market. If we had been on the second floor of our house, we could have seen them. Our pleasure at seeing American soldiers was short-lived as hours passed without us seeing another American and night was approaching. We assumed that the Japanese soldiers in the Balagtas Apartments had seen us talking to the Americans and we were very afraid of what the night would bring. Despite knowing the American patrol was a few yards to the north of us in the yard across the street, we also knew that we were still in Japanese territory and the Americans were probably at least a block away to the South. So the men in our group were assigned to various shifts to stand guard during the night at different points in the yard where we thought the Japanese might approach. Of course, all we had were sticks and small knives, but at least we would not be surprised. However, the night passed by without incident. (I must make sure that the reader understands that while the day and night are passing, there still is a lot of gunfire going on all around us, the American soldiers and the Japanese soldiers are still fighting house to house, and the American artillery shells are continuing to land around the Stadiums a block away. Additionally, during the night, flares are dropping at regular intervals in the vicinity of Vito Cruz, the big street in front of the Stadiums and 1 block away from us.) I'm not sure why they needed flares because there were so many fires going on around us that the night wasn't dark at all. You could even read under the glare. Imagine life going on while a battle is being waged right next to you, in the streets and the yards around you, and there is nothing that you can do.

The next morning, the 13th, another American patrol showed up. This one consisted of only 3 men and belonged to the 11th Airborne. Later in the afternoon about 30 Americans occupied the American School building on Donada Street. The Japanese had tried to demolish the school by burning it, but the damage wasn't much since it was built with concrete. We contacted these soldiers, learned they were quite thirsty, and took them some water from a good well behind Judge Moran's destroyed house on Menlo. The Japanese must have found out that there were several American soldiers at the American School so their artillery and mortars in the Stadiums started shelling the school. So now we had to run for cover from the Japanese artillery. Fortunately, the Japanese shelling wasn't very heavy, about 1 shell for every 10 American shells we had dodged the previous days. All day long the Americans shelled the Stadiums and towards evening it got even stronger. The noise of the whistle of the shell and the explosion got to be so common that we ignored it and even got to the point of hardly taking any notice. Meanwhile, the Japanese in the Stadiums continued shelling us, primarily with mortars, since they knew the American troops were in our vicinity. All during the day there were still fires all around us. The sun wasn't yellow; it was bright red. An American officer showed up shortly before dark and, after looking at the ridiculous shelter we had, suggested we move south behind the American lines. He said that since we were in the range of both the American and Japanese artillery, it was too dangerous to stay. It was very difficult for our group to decide. Some picked up and left while others decided to stay. Shortly after, an American sergeant came over the wall and advised us to stay put since night was almost upon us and in the night we would be exposed to Japanese snipers and the Americans had been told to shoot at anything that moved. So we just stayed. By this time we were also getting pretty tired of lugging ourselves and our stuff over walls and we couldn't expose ourselves to the street. Besides the street had those tank traps and land mines. Those remaining posted guards during the night. While the shelling got heavier during the night, no shells exploded nearby. However, lots of shell splinters dropped around us but nobody was hit. Now we were in American territory with the Stadiums a block away in Japanese territory and we weren't sure who controlled the block directly across the street between us and the Stadiums. However, we did know that there were still Japanese soldiers/snipers there and in our area.

Early the following morning, the 14th, a patrol came to us and asked us again if we knew were the Japanese had planted mines. Some of us went with them over the walls to show them the places we knew. We watched them using their knives to dig the ground around the mine and then remove

the mine. We told them of other mines on Leveriza and Donada Streets but no one could get at them since the Japanese snipers in the Stadiums and Harrison Park covered that portion of the roads.

Heavy fighting was now going on around the Stadiums, a block away. The door-to-door fighting in our block had now stopped and the Americans were concentrating their heavy guns and mortars on the Stadiums. The Americans moved several artillery pieces into the American School. The fighting was especially fierce for the basketball and baseball stadiums facing Vito Cruz. For days the Americans had been pounding the Stadiums with artillery. We were still living in the open garage with a tin roof. Often the shrapnel from the shelling as well as pieces of the Stadiums' concrete walls would hit our tin roof. By now the Japanese artillery had been silenced so we did not have to fear any shells exploding in the yard where we were. (Days later when my father had

A closer look at the Legislative Building.

a chance to do an inspection trip around the Stadiums, he noticed several destroyed Japanese artillery pieces in the Stadiums as well as Harrison Park, on Cortabitarte Street, Dewey Boulevard and the Yacht Club).

News came to us that the American troops had now worked their way from Santa Ana and had now reached Vito Cruz/Taft Avenue. Once the Americans had cleared Leveriza of land mines and had repaired the tank traps, tanks started to rumble down Leveriza on the way to the Stadiums. What a sight to watch them go right by you! On the 17th, after days of shelling, the Stadiums were finally cleared of Japanese soldiers as tanks broke through the walls. We no longer had to be silent when moving around. On the 18th, the Filipino families in the area that were still alive and living in open garages, moved to other houses they had on the other side of the Pasig River, where they had experienced no destruction. We also wanted to get out but we didn't have anywhere to go. And we couldn't go far since the suitcases we had were too heavy to carry any distance and even if we could get a push cart, we feared there were land mines in the road. So we decided to move to a house on Fresno Street that was owned by a friend of ours, Mr. Henry Bauman, who with his family had been interned. The house was in good condition since it was concrete. The houses on the South side were made of wood and so burned down, while many of the houses on the North side were made of concrete. So once again, we gathered our total possessions and climbed over several walls. There was no furniture in the house; it had all been looted. We used a lantern we had to get around at night. We found out the next day that we were the only family living on the entire Fresno Road. We were consistently scared sleeping at night because of this. For the next few days hardly anyone ever passed by on Fresno Road. At night we watched the flares that were falling in the Malate district and in the bay near the Boulevard. While we knew there were about 100 American soldiers at the American School a little over a half block away, we still didn't have any real sense of security. We still had to watch out for Japanese snipers in the area. Fully a week after we had moved to these new quarters, 3 Japanese soldiers entered the Chinese man's house (his house was made with concrete so it was only partially burned) at about 1 a.m. They made the people cook rice for them and after eating it, left without doing anybody any harm. I realize that they didn't want to make any noise and announce their presence to the American soldiers near by. Two nights later 5 Japanese soldiers entered Mrs. Whitney's house just across the street were we had lived. A few days before Mrs. Filer had moved in there since her house had been burned. The Japanese asked for food and left after about 30 minutes without doing any harm. All of this happened after the Stadiums were in American hands and the fighting was going on further away in the Ermita district. And we were in American territory. A couple of days later, some Filipinos found a Japanese soldier in the Balagtas Apartments. They skinned him alive.

Then a whole bunch of American troops moved into what was left of the Stadiums and we felt a lot safer. The fighting moved further and further away. The house to house fighting continued. But it took days of fighting to take the main Japanese fortress, the Walled City. It was about March 1st when the Walled City was finally taken.

The South of Manila from the Pasay Market to the Pasig River and from Paco market to the Manila Bay was completely wiped out. There was hardly a house still standing and those which were, were made of concrete and badly damaged. The Government buildings were heavily damaged, as were most of the apartment complexes. I have heard that Manila was the 2nd or 3rd worst destroyed Allied city in WWII—Warsaw and then either Rotterdam or Manila. I have no idea how valid that is. There were no trees left in our area and no shade to walk in. All the apartment houses in Malate and Ermita were burnt out, though still standing. Several days after the fighting was over, my father went to see what damage had been done in the Ermita district but turned back after he reached the intersection of Mabini and Herran. From Cortabitarte down to Herran/Mabini he walked through ruins. It was practically level all over with dead civilians and Japanese soldiers lying all around, most of them partly burnt. He did not meet a single person or a stray dog. He said he then turned back since it was just too eerie and he was afraid to go on.

After the Americans had taken the Stadiums (the fighting was still going on but much further away and we thought we were fairly safe), my father and I went to see if any of our friends had survived and what the damage to our area had been. Most of the houses had been burnt and little remained standing. It was my turn to see the dead bodies all around us; in the yards, on the sidewalks and along the street. By now they were starting to smell pretty badly as the sun had done its work decaying them. Additionally, the flies and the maggots were all over them as they rotted. You dared not touch any since the Japanese had booby-trapped some. There were no dogs or cats left. Either they had been killed by shrapnel, burnt or killed for food. I looked for Billy Conn, a friend with whom I had played during the war and who lived a few blocks away. He had not survived. We found some dead friends but not others. Those you didn't find, you didn't know whether they had been burned beyond recognition, had been killed somewhere else, or had survived because they had been elsewhere. Most of the people on Balagtas Street were murdered and in Pax Court, Mrs. Stahl survived

(she played dead and the Japanese thought she was dead) but was badly burned. There was a Chinese family living just west of Pax Court. The father had gone to Santa Ana to obtain medicine he desperately needed for one of his kids and was there on February 11th. When he tried to get back, he couldn't because American soldiers suddenly were around him and shooting at the Japanese. Days later when the Stadiums were taken, he came home only to find his whole family, wife and 7 children had been murdered by the Japanese. (This less than a block away from where we were hiding.) The Foxes next door to them (on the other side from where we were hiding) were never seen again.

Nearly all the families and their servants on Vito Cruz were murdered. The Swiss Community lost 25 people and it wasn't a big community to start with. But it was hard to tell how many people in our area survived since the ones that had escaped the fires, the Japanese shooting, the Japanese bayoneting and the American shelling were Filipinos and had scattered in all directions, probably seeking relatives. However, we know that very few civilians in our area survived. There were just too many dead and partially-burnt dead people in our neighbors' houses and yards.

Walking around our neighborhood was like a scene from a movie. Besides the bodies and the destroyed houses, there were many destroyed Japanese artillery pieces, not only on the grounds of Harrison Park but also on Cortabitarte, the Boulevard and the Yacht Club. We later learned that there wasn't much left of the University of the Philippines. The Philippine General Hospital was heavily damaged and partly burnt. The Japanese had machine guns in the corridors of the hospital and the Americans had to use artillery to get them out. Most churches were in ruin and the civilians who had sought "safe" shelter in them were killed. Fifteen priests at La Salle College were murdered along with the many civilians who had sought refuge in that religious place. The Japanese simply mowed people down in the corridors and rooms. Men, women and children were all killed. There were many, many accounts of babies being tossed into the air and then caught on bayonets. Our friend Father Kelly of the Remedios Church and hospital was also murdered. (He was a fixture in front of the hospital smoking a cigar.)

Hundreds of civilians bled to death during the shelling. There were no doctors and even if there had been, there was no way a doctor could get to them. The Japanese shot anybody they could find or saw moving. Some died from minor shell splinters when they could not stem the blood flow and the wound could not be shut. Others died from starvation.

The bodies lay around for days. There were just too many of them to bury and the ones that did get buried, were often buried right where they lay or in back yards, in empty lots and even on the Boulevard. Some probably had relatives that could have come looking for them, but the relatives might have been killed as well. Thousands died in the burning houses with little or no trace left of them. When the fighting for the Walled City was over, about 3000 women and children were found, but only 5 old men. No additional men were found in that district by the time we left and that was 5 weeks after the fighting was over. The houses left standing, because either the Japanese did not get around to burning them or that were made of concrete, were looted. Looters were right behind the advancing American soldiers and took everything that was left in the houses and apartments. Bathroom fixtures, toilets, Fridgidaires, bathtubs, everything was gone. Houses that came through the fighting only partially damaged, disappeared within a few days if the owner didn't show up. The looters took the wooden floors, walls, and

ceilings away to build small shacks for themselves or they used the planks for firewood which was very scarce. Lots of these houses were owned by the Americans and British interned during the war. I don't think anyone has written about this aspect of the battle for Manila.

When we went over to look at our house, it was burnt to the ground. Not a wall was left standing. Everything was lost. We sifted through the ashes and did find five Setsuma porcelain vases. How those managed to survive the intense heat and the falling from the second floor to the ground, I will never know. They are presently sitting in my living room. Oddly, the servant quarters and garage did not burn, although the furniture and the walls were battered full of holes by shell explosions and shrapnel. We did still have our mattresses, mosquito nets and a couple of kitchen utensils in our new location. My parents' nineteen years of married life had gone up in flames. 10 trunks of things that we had been saving for the Loucks, Forsters and other friends that were interned in Santo Tomas were also burnt. The irony of it was that these were burnt after those families had already been liberated by the Americans.

In spite of all the days of shelling we had endured, the gunfire all around us and the Japanese killing everyone they saw, the family of the three of us and Valentina had survived. Most of our neighbors had not. (In October, Valentina finally got to get back to her home in Balaoan. Upon her arrival, she found out that both her parents, her sister and her brother-in-law were killed by the Japanese.)

By this time we were out of food. We still could get water from the wells in the area. But we went hungry for several days. When you see movies of war-torn areas, you often see those dirty, bedraggled little kids with their hands out pleading with the GIs for

Devastated Paco District of Manila, March 1945 (courtesy F. Baldassarre)

food. Well, that was me. My parents had it worse, since being parents, what food they had went to the child first. I think my father was now down to about 97 pounds. You certainly could see a lot of bone and you could see bones on me. One time a GI gave me his K rations, which I ate quickly and eagerly. I threw up. My stomach could not tolerate that "rich" food. (Many years later I was drafted into the US Army. I had a hard time eating those tasteless, yucky K rations.)

I was a kid. I did not fully realize the seriousness of the whole situation. I was taking part in a "war game". I did what I was told to do. My parents, on the other hand, had to be terrified most of the time. Life and death decisions had to be made. And some of them quickly. Any one of their decisions could have ended with death. How do you portion what food you have left; for how many days;

when can you go get some water from a well; where are the Japanese soldiers; in which yards. We could have been seen; could have been heard; a shell could have hit us directly; shrapnel could have hit us and we could have bled to death; we could have been in the wrong yard at the wrong time; we could have been in our house when the Japanese came into our yard; why did the two Japanese soldiers who found us, not kill us? Why did we survive while our neighbors did not?

And what a prospect my parents faced. No house, no food, no money (Japanese occupation money was now worthless), no job. No relatives close by to help. And no prospects. In your mid-to-late forties, after 19 years of married life, and you have to start all over again from scratch. They certainly must have had a sense of hopelessness. But at least we were alive.

PART 4

WAR AND PEACE

CHAPTER VIII

AFTER THE LIBERATION

JUERGEN GOLDHAGEN'S NARRATIVE

The day after the first GIs came through, the Peters asked if they could stay with us until their own house had been repaired. We welcomed them and they stayed with us for a week or two. Then, the Weigerts appeared and also asked if they could stay with us for a short while till they could find a place to stay. They had walked from the Philippine General Hospital, where they had been liberated, to their rental house near us, but that house had been damaged in some fighting. So, they walked on until they came to us and were delighted that our house was still intact. We had Mom and Dad and me, Mr. Lienhard, Mr. and Mrs. Peter, Hans and Vreneli, and Mr. Helmut Weigert and his mother and father all staying with us. We had mattresses on the living room floor and somehow we all made do.

The Peters told us that just before the Japanese pulled out the soldiers had come to kill the Gutierrezes and would have killed anyone with them, i.e. the Peters. The Gutierrezes had helped the guerillas and the Japanese suspected them. Fortunately, both families had gone into their well-concealed air-raid shelter as the fighting neared their area, and the Japanese didn't find them.

It was great having the Peters with us because Hans was like a brother to me. One morning, we all went to the small-arms ammo dump and as we sat there looking at the wide assortment of ammo, we could hear shells whistling overhead. We assumed that they were American shells on their way to hit the Japanese. We tried to see the shells in the air, but couldn't.

Speaking of shelling, about one week after we had been liberated, there were some loud explosions one evening and we lay down on the floor of the living room. The Japanese were shelling our area. The next morning, we heard that Mr. Prieur had been killed and we were stunned. It turned out that one of the first shells had landed in his backyard, where he had a small repair shop. They were upstairs in their house at the time and he told them to go into the cellar, the one where we had all sheltered when the Japanese blew up the ammunition. His wife begged him to go into the cellar with them, but he claimed there wouldn't be any more shells and he had to go see what damage had been done to his repair shop. Almost immediately, another shell landed and blew his head off. We civilians had no idea about shelling and didn't know that several shells would usually come after the first one. Neho and Gaston were extremely upset and, though they had wished their father dead many times because he was very strict with them, they took back all their words, but it was too late.

The shelling was the most terrifying event of the war for me, even worse than the air raids and bombs. There was nothing to watch, nor time to prepare. Just a whistle and then an explosion. The Japanese must have been trying to shell the junction of the three main highways near us, i.e., España Extension, Santa Mesa Blvd. and the Circumferential Road. A GI told us that the US Army was trying to destroy the Japanese artillery, but it was a gun in a tunnel and only came out at night. The shelling continued with a few shells a night for about three nights before the Americans finally silenced the guns.

Mr. Prieur and a Filipino grandmother were the only casualties that I knew of in our area. The grandmother, who ironically lived near the Prieurs, was in an air-raid shelter and a GI saw her face peeking out. He told her to come out, but she ducked back. The next time she peeked out the GI shot her in the head. He thought she was a Japanese and was very sad when he realized what had happened, but he couldn't take any chances with his own life.

Electricity and water were the other casualties, and they had

Juergen Goldhagen in 1945.

occurred on February 4, when the Japanese blew up their ammunition. At night, we had candle light or just sat in the dark and watched flares shoot up during the battle for Manila. I got water to flush our toilets from a nearby creek. We got drinking water from a well near the Cubao City Hall, about three blocks away, and then we had to boil it before using it to make sure it was safe. We used a little pushcart that we loaded with what containers we had. The water supply was soon restored, but the electricity took several months.

For several days, Hans Peter and I would go to our ammo dump and bring home rifle ammo and bandoliers. Among the ammo, we found clips for American M-1 Garand rifles, material which the Japanese had captured after the fall of Bataan and Corregidor. Hans and I didn't know what the clips were, but later I found out when some of my GI friends showed me their M-1s. We also took home unused Japanese flares that were in that dump. The flares were in a can and when you took them out they had parachutes attached. We would take the flares off and then tie a stone to the parachute strings, throw the stone into the air, and watch it float down. Very nice toys. We couldn't read the Japanese instructions on how to light the flares, but that was just as well.

I used to like handling the fuses because they were really pretty and had an element of danger. One type was cone-shaped with a push-down top. I could see it had a two-pronged pin through the fuse near its top and I figured that was a safety pin, so I never took the pin out when I pushed the plunger down. The pin could be easily pulled out or pushed back in. I thought of pulling the pin out and then dropping the fuse over a low wall to see if it would go off. The only thing that stopped me was that if I dropped it over the wall and it didn't go off, what would I do then? So I never tried it.

121

Another kind of fuse had some numbers on a wide, round base, and then a long rounded metal tube sticking out of the base. In the middle of the underside of the base was a slot, and you could insert a screwdriver there and move the slot to a certain number. I was very leery of that type of fuse, believing it could blow up in my hands if I used a screwdriver, and I never messed with it.

Another type of gunpowder we found in the fields was made up of long thin rods with a hollow middle, like a long piece of spaghetti. We found these near the large shell casings that I had carried home, and we quickly learned that if you lit a bundle of the rods, they burned nice and slow. If you lit a single rod, however, it would start to burn and then would emit a pop and break in two.

The best effect was that if you broke off a small piece and lit it, it would streak off like a little rocket. Such fun! We all played with them and showed them to anyone who didn't know about them. It was the start of the dry season, so there was never any rain to ruin all the ammo lying around. One day, one of the kids we had demonstrated the little rockets to took home a bundle to play with. A few days later, I learned that he had put the bundle at his feet, lit a small piece of a rod, and it darted away, but came back, and then went right into the bundle at his feet, causing it to catch fire. The kid got some bad burns and ended up in a hospital.

One evening, shortly after being liberated, we had some GIs visiting us when one of them heard a noise outside our window. They immediately motioned us to the floor and one of them cocked his tommy-gun and was ready for action. Fortunately, it proved to be a false alarm.

The Egeas had two beautiful daughters and an open patio, and before long the officers would have parties at their house and also at ours. While we didn't have any beautiful daughters, Mom was a terrific cook, so some of the officers would bring food over, which Mom would prepare. Then there would be good food, music, and a homey atmosphere, which meant a lot to the guys. They also enjoyed talking to us as much as we enjoyed talking to them.

Yes, we had phonograph music, mostly from V-discs that the officers brought along with their phonograph. Thanks to the generosity of a Major Dorie, the Egeas got a portable Army generator, which was wired up to provide electricity for all of the four houses the Egeas owned, including ours. The generator was donated because the officers liked having parties and dancing to music on the patio, which was decorated with colored light bulbs. Electricity is such a wonderful gift.

About a week after we had been liberated, some GIs visited the Egeas and parked their jeep in the open garage. They had a machine gun mounted on the jeep and while they were in the house, I was tempted to climb up and fire the gun, but I figured it would be too noisy, and who knows what would have happened, so I didn't. Besides, had I climbed up and tried, I wouldn't have known how to load the gun.

U.S. Army tent camps sprang up in the fields around us and I had a wonderful time visiting the GIs and watching movies on outdoor screens. I had no trouble getting into any of the camps and, at one point, I was going to a different camp movie every night. There was a big camp in the field next to our old Green House and I spent so much time there that when they closed to civilians, they gave me a special pass so that I could still visit my friends.

The camps were made up of twelve-man tents with wooden floors, and the GIs slept on cots with mosquito netting. I loved visiting the GIs and made many friends. Best of all, they would feed me. Someone would hand me a mess kit and then I would stand in the chow line and have it filled. I liked most of the food and particularly the canned fruit cocktail for dessert, but I soon got tired of dehydrated potatoes and powdered eggs.

At home, we had trouble buying food because all the supply lines were disrupted. After the first days of our liberation, we were so hungry that my Dad and Mr. Peter went to one of the camps and begged for food from one of the officers. That kind gentleman gave them a case of corned beef hash and a case of canned pilchards. At first, we thought they were great, but after a few days we got tired of them. At least, we weren't going to starve.

A short while later, ration centers were opened up and one could get free rice and canned goods. Dad and I went to them several times. At one, we saw a GI with his shirt off and he had several scars that he claimed were from fighting the Japanese. He was a big strong guy and I certainly believed him. One evening Mom, Dad and I were invited to have supper at a small airstrip and, just as we were about to eat, they flashed an air-raid alert. They told us that there was a Japanese plane nearby and two P-38s took off. I loved the excitement, but I was scared that the Japanese were going to come back and beat the Americans again, as in 1941. I had no idea of how strong the Americans were in 1945.

To this day, I still regret something that happened to me when I visited a group of GIs. One of them had just gotten a big box of hard candy from home and told me to take as many as I wanted. So, I took just about all the red ones, taking some for myself and some for my friends. When I visited him the next day he asked me if I had taken all the red ones. I said "No," and he called me a liar and said he didn't want me coming back into the tent again. Another guy said he believed me, and I was welcome to come back any time and that the guy with the candy was just a mean guy. I was so afraid of getting punished that I lied and took the easy way out. I couldn't think to tell him that my friends and I hadn't had any candy for three years. Yes, the Japanese patrol that had marched past us had thrown us some hard candy, and while it was sweet, it had no flavor.

The closest friends I made were a bunch of guys in a radar and searchlight unit that had moved into the partly finished house one block away from us, which had been occupied by the Japanese and from which we used to hear them shout when they did their morning exercises.

One afternoon, as I was on my way home, I passed the house and a GI from the upper floor yelled from a window, "Hey, kid, come on in here." They asked what I was doing and found it hard to believe that I had lived through the Japanese occupation. They adopted me and I spent most of each day at their house, returning home only for lunch. Often, they fed me in the evenings, and I really liked that. Especially when they had fried chicken. Boy, was that food good! I did think it strange that they ate at 5:30 p.m. instead of at 8:00 p.m. as we did, but I quickly adjusted.

I would talk with the GIs and play card games with them such as casino and hearts, both of which they taught me. We also played rummy, and thanks to a lot of rummy games with Mom, I had card sense and was able to hold my own against the guys. They also played cribbage, but I didn't learn that.

123

I read anything I could get my hands on: their copes of *Time*, *Life*, *Saturday Evening Post*, *Colliers*, and *Reader's Digest*. They were overseas editions for servicemen, were printed on light paper, and didn't have any ads. There was also *Yank*, the GI magazine, and specially sized books that could fit into a field pack or fatigue pants side pockets. The books were of all different types, and I would pick and choose what I wanted to read.

All in all, I was having a great time, but the war was still going on and there was still lots of fighting in areas further removed from us. One day, I was walking down the highway with a GI when a weapons carrier truck went speeding down the road. The guy was driving really fast and had a load in the back made up of several boots sticking out from beneath a tarp. I asked the guy I was with why the fellow was driving so fast, and my friend told me that the truck was carrying dead GIs and the guy was driving fast to keep the smell from reaching him. A very depressing sight.

I guess one of the reasons I was so popular with the GIs was that most of them were homesick and I reminded them of kids they knew back home or of the kids that most of them had just been.

One of the guys from the radar unit saw one of the parachute flares that I had and asked if I knew where they were some more. Sure I did, and I gladly took him there. We gathered about half a dozen and then put them into the small hollow under one of the empty drums the GIs boiled water in for cleaning their mess gear. Normally, gasoline would be poured into the hollow, then lit, and it would boil the water in the drum. This time, we poured some gasoline over the flares, ran a small trail of gasoline to the doorway where we were standing, and then my friend applied a match. There was a wonderful display of pyrotechnics as

the flares went whoosh and caught fire. The only trouble was that there were so many of them that flaming particles flew through the air, one of them rolling off the two of us as we held each other in surprise. The sergeant in charge of the outfit told me that if I ever came in with another flare he wouldn't let me near the place again. So, I never brought in another one.

In the back of that house was a large adobe stone-lined hole, which may have been made for a swimming pool that was never completed. It was filled with dirty rainwater and had tadpoles and frogs swimming in it. Just for fun, some of the GIs would throw me into it. My having learned to swim in the shallow rain puddle two years before stood me in good stead and I enjoyed my swim in the filthy water. Mom didn't like it at all when I would get home soaking wet. She threatened to prohibit me from going there anymore if they continued to throw me in. When I told them about the threat, they stopped.

I saw some hand grenades in one of their rooms, and I wanted to take one and throw it in the pool to see what it would do and what it would sound like. I never asked and so I never got to do it. Most probably they would have let me.

They had a radar set that they had to operate during the day and night. They let me sit there a few times and look at the scope, but I found it pretty boring. They told me it was all top secret and in any pictures that they took of each other they could never show any part of the radar set or the picture would be confiscated by the censor.

The unit also had a searchlight tied into the radar set. One night, I was taking a shower in my house and they shone the light at the window. I thought the bulb in the bathroom had burst. When I realized what it was I jumped to the window and waved at my buddies. I had told them where the shower window was.

Thanks to all the GI food I was getting, I started to grow taller. And the guys even managed to get me a pair of Army boots because I didn't have a pair of decent shoes. I loved them and used to put waterproof dubbing on them. Mom hated to see me wear them because I would walk with a slouch, the boots being rather heavy.

Besides all the camps around us, we had Brigadier General Spence from the 38th Division renting the two rooms from us that Mr. Lienhard used to live in. They were two rooms in a row, one being a sitting room and the other a bedroom, and they opened onto the upstairs porch from which we used to watch the air raids. The rooms had an unobstructed view to the west and the famous Manila sunsets. Mr. Lienhard was still with us and moved into another room in our house. At that time, he had no job and no money, but we still let him stay with us without charge. He had been so helpful to us all through the Occupation and we weren't about to kick him out on the street.

Lt. Robert Tewksbury, aide-de-camp to General Spence told us that our names had been selected because my Dad had helped the guerillas a lot, and so we were on a special list the US Army had to help such people. Dad never talked to me about helping the guerillas, but I was glad the general did move in with us. He didn't stay with us much, but the rooms were his to use whenever he wanted. It was only for a few months, but the rental income was a big help. He left a blue U.S. Navy bedspread with us, much nicer than a drab Army blanket.

Lt. Tewksbury was from Indiana and he became a very good friend of the family. Once, he invited me to spend a weekend at the Division's camp further out in the country, sleeping on cots and in a tent. I had a wonderful time. At one point, we had some target practice with the .30 caliber carbine, shooting at some tin cans. Somehow, I knocked two of them over with one shot and we couldn't figure out how that happened. The two cans were side by side, so the bullet must have split in two or ricocheted somehow. We were all very surprised.

After target practice, we gave the carbines to a GI to clean. I told him that I hoped it wasn't too much trouble and he said, "No, not at all." Most probably, he owed Bob a favor or Bob had paid him to do it. Bob had told my parents that when I was ready to come to the States that I should write him a letter and he would act as my sponsor. At that time, a sponsor had to put up a $10,000 bond or some type of similar guarantee that I would not become a liability of the US Government, should I run out of money.

Five years later, in 1950, I wrote Bob that I had finished high school and was ready to come to the States. He put up the guarantee and I was able to immigrate to the States. Unfortunately, Bob died in a scuba accident in the mid-70s, but I will never forget his kindness.

Once, Mom was desperate for some cigarettes and smoked a pack of the general's Old Gold cigarettes. Then, she hit the panic button because she got word that the general was going to arrive in a day or so and she didn't have any replacement pack. Mom thought that she'd have a few days and some GI would give her a pack of Old Gold. Well, during that time, a GI did give her a pack of Chesterfields, but not Old Gold. I knew that I could find a GI among the many camps I went to who would swap them for Old Gold, Old Gold not being as popular as Chesterfields. Sure enough, I was able to do it easily enough much to my Mom's relief.

A bulletin I read on the notice board at the radar unit alerted me to the danger of the percussion cap on an unfired rifle round. One could lose an eye from flying metal if one tried to hammer a nail onto the cap. That may also be why I never kept a Japanese artillery fuse. Very pretty to look at, but I didn't know how to render them harmless.

A short way away from us on my small bike and near the Bonifacio monument on the Circumferential Road, there was a small airstrip made from Marsten mats. These mats were strips of steel with holes punched in them, which could be joined together to make a runway out of any flat area. I would bike there and watch the activity.

Most of the time, they were loading the wounded onto C-46s, which was a huge

plane in my eyes. One day I saw a Piper Cub L-4, which had lettering painted on it that showed it had been paid for by war bonds bought by kids from some high school in the States. I thought how nice that was and how I wished I could be in the States.

One morning, someone let me get into the cockpit of a P-61 Black Widow night fighter and I really enjoyed it. What an array of instruments! They also had some B-25s parked there. Then, one morning, I got there early and watched a pilot talking to an officer by the side of the runway where I was standing. The pilot got into his P-51 Mustang, took off, flew back, and then buzzed us. He dove so low that I was about to jump into the ditch beside us when he finally pulled up. Terrific!

Another P-51 pilot was not so lucky. One morning, I was still at home when there was a really loud whistle followed by an

The Finance Building in 1945.

explosion. My first thought was that a shell had landed nearby, but no, it was a P-51. The pilot, along with some others, had buzzed the house the Peters had moved into temporarily. This one went too low, hit some trees, and crashed his plane. There were pieces of aircraft scattered over a large area and the pilot's body ended up a block away from our house. I jumped on my bike and hurried to the end of our block, where I saw a group of Army men and then a parachute and the boots of the pilot sticking out from underneath. I didn't stay to watch any further.

A week or two after our liberation, we went with the Peters to look at their house on Manga Street off of Santa Mesa Boulevard. Just as we got there, the strap on my bakya, or wooden shoe, broke and I had to be carried piggy-back around their yard. I couldn't walk barefoot because there were shell fragments all over the place. The Japanese had built a concrete pill box with an anti-tank gun overlooking Santa Mesa Boulevard and I learned later that it had knocked out three American tanks before it got knocked out. The Japanese gun was still in place, but it had been hit by American shells and the inside was a mess of torn-up gun and concrete. We didn't see any bodies in it.

We did see a dead Japanese lying on top of the concrete over the septic tank around the back of the house. He was lying on his back and I asked someone to get his helmet for me. Mr. Peter went and started to lift it off the man's head when some maggots fell out. Disgusted at the maggots and seeing that the helmet was the wicker type and not a steel helmet, I told Mr. Peter to leave it alone. Luckily, it wasn't booby trapped, or the Americans had already removed any booby traps, because we didn't know anything about the Japanese booby-trapping their dead. Had it been, Mr. Peter would have been seriously injured or killed.

The Americans had also put up white cloth tapes along sections of the yard. At the time, we didn't know what that meant, (but now I know it meant that it was safe to walk within the areas of the tapes and that outside them there would be unexploded shells or mines). Fortunately, we stayed within the tape-marked walkways. Perhaps the Peters had been told and knew it. I certainly didn't.

Earlier, I had seen similar tapes along a path at the end of our street, but I walked down the path anyway, having done so many times in the past. On either side of the path were unexploded Japanese shells from their attempt to blow up their ammunition. About a year later, there were still clusters of unused mortar rounds lying along the roadways and I was tempted to take some home, but never did. They were too common. When the rice had been harvested and the farmers set fire to the fields to refertilize the soil, some of the shells would explode. As far as I know, no one got killed by them, though a few roofs got shrapnel holes in them.

I used to get lots of candy from the GIs. The first troops would give me the gum from their C-rations and it was usually a stick or two of Juicy Fruit or Spearmint. Later, someone gave me a whole box of Beeman's pepsin-flavored gum, which I wasn't fond of, but a whole box was riches indeed. I really liked Blackjack gum, but I didn't get that too often. Once, someone gave me a can of Charms sourballs and they were terrific. I particularly liked the clear ones that were apple-flavored.

For quite a while, we had to boil our drinking water, but the GIs had large canvas bags called Lister bags. These would be filled with water and some chemicals were added to purify it. At the bottom of the bag were tiny faucets from which they would fill their canteens or canteen cups. I used to drink their water when I got thirsty, but I didn't like it because of the chemical taste.

From the American Red Cross, my folks got me a cloth jacket with leather sleeves that I would wear to the evening movies that the GIs had in the open fields. Outdoors, it got cool in February and March. The jacket was a bit small, but it kept me warm and I was grateful to the unknown U.S. family that had donated it.

Because at first we had no electricity, some of the GIs gave me a flashlight or two. Some of my playmates also had some and we had a grand time trying to see whose flashlight could shine farthest. We scrounged batteries from our Army friends, but the batteries never lasted very long because of the humidity in the tropics and because we played around with them so much.

A few times, I saw some Army trucks go by full of Japanese POWs. One of the GIs told me he couldn't understand why the Filipinos would throw stones at them because the POWs were now harmless. I thought the Japanese were getting what they deserved even though they hadn't done us any harm.

Shortly after April 1945, the radar unit left for the United States. I know it was after April because when President Roosevelt died they were still in the house. I remember running home to tell Mom and Dad about Roosevelt's death. I cried like a baby when the guys left. I was so fond of them. Particularly Mike Cikusa and Donald Porcaro. Mike gave me a Japanese rifle when he left, and the neighborhood kids and I all played at being soldiers with the rifles the GIs had given us. While Japanese small-arms ammo was readily available in the

dumps around us, we had the good sense not to load the rifles. We had all seen what war was really like and we didn't want to hurt each other with those guns.

Another group of GIs moved into the house, but they were different from the radar unit men and I never got that friendly with them. Then, a whole bunch of trucks moved into the empty field next to the radar unit's house and set up camp. It was interesting how quickly they did it. The trucks roared in, stopped, the tenting equipment was pulled out, and before long another camp had been set up. The truckers were from Europe, where the war had ended, and they were now going to continue to fight against Japan. All they wanted to do was to go home, but they didn't have enough points to do so. I became friendly with some of the guys, but not as friendly as with the radar unit men. Perhaps that was because I was leery of getting hurt again, knowing that these guys would also leave some day.

The truckers had some German souvenirs and one of them showed me a pistol he would give me. I went home and asked my folks permission to have a gun and they said O.K. The next day when I went to get it, the guy told me he had sold it to some other GI. He offered me a German army belt buckle instead, but I wasn't having any of that. He had promised me a gun and I wasn't going to be placated with a belt buckle.

Another camp sprung up at the other end of our street and those men had also come from Europe. Some of them guessed that I came from Germany. Prior to them, the GIs would always guess that I came from the States when I challenged them to guess where I was from. These guys, having served in Germany, recognized a trace of a German accent in my speech. I found that hard to believe because I didn't think I had any at all.

One evening, Mr. Bruno Deutschkrohn and his son Werner took Dad and me to a movie in Manila, driving a US Army command car they had bought. On the way home, we passed another command car driven by two soldiers and they nearly cut us off. Then, they pulled over and let us pass them and then they started after us again. We passed and repassed each other until just before we got to our turnoff. At that point, they clipped us and we swerved off of España Extension and started to tip over. Luckily, we hit the adobe wall outside of Rosenda L. Benitez's house and our command car righted itself. I was sitting in the middle of the front seat and thought we were going to turn completely over. It happened so fast I didn't have time to be afraid.

Soon, an MP jeep came along, but as civilians we weren't familiar with the Army identification numbering system, so we couldn't give them any information about the other car. Since there wasn't any damage to the Benitez's wall, we didn't wake them up. They had a boy older than I who I used to play with during the Occupation, but what I really liked were the books and magazines they had. That was where I got my first exposure to the *Reader's Digest*, which I still enjoy.

Around March, St. Joseph's Academy, a Catholic school, opened and I was put into the sixth grade. I would hitchhike to and from school and for a while some GIs in a jeep gave me a regular ride to school at about 7:30. One morning, as I walked down to the corner of España Extension and New York Avenue for my ride, I saw some white smoke, and as I got to the corner I saw a Filipino lying face down on New York Avenue on the other side of España Extension. He was lying across an electric wire with the smoke coming out of his body. As I watched, part of his body burst into flame, and one of his legs bent at the

knee and curled onto the back of his thigh. Luckily, the smoke was blowing the other way and I didn't have to smell it.

At that point, my ride came and I went to school, wondering what had happened. That afternoon, when I visited the camp by the Green House, a GI guard told me that very early in the morning the wire had been hanging low over the road. A jeep had come along, and one of the GIs in it leaned out of the jeep and lifted the wire over it so they could drive on. The jeep tires had insulated him and nothing had happened. The Filipino, who may have seen that nothing happened to the GI, came along and when he touched the wire that was the end of him. He wasn't insulated from the ground, and in fact he was the ground. Poor guy.

Things were getting more normal now and I wasn't able to get rides from GIs as easily as before. One time, Mom needed some medicine from the city and I told her I would hitch-hike both ways. She insisted on my taking enough money in case I needed to get a ride. I had no trouble getting a ride in on the back of a truck, but on the way home I just couldn't hitch a ride. As it was getting dark, I finally had to take a jitney and pay for the ride with Mom's money. Jitneys were jeeps that Filipinos had converted into small six-passenger carriers by extending the back of a jeep. Usually, the driver and two passengers sat up front and four people sat facing each other in the back. There wasn't much room, but they were cheap and stopped for passengers wherever they were flagged down. Nothing like a regular schedule or a designated stop. (They are still in use in Manila, are colorfully painted and decorated, and have become a symbol of the city.)

One day, Mrs. Peter wanted to visit Santo Tomas and I volunteered to help her hitch-hike there. When we got there, I looked up

Mrs. Cummings, who used to live in Pax Court, when we were there. I saw the nipa shack she had lived in and I thought it was rather nice. I didn't go into the main building where other internees were housed. I did see a lot of GIs and a US armored car that was interesting, but there I was just another kid among many and I didn't know any of them. I was glad when I got back home among my own circle of friends.

An officer friend of my family had given us a ride to Santo Tomas, but hitch-hiking home was tough. No one would pick us up and I kept thinking if Mrs. Peter had been a beautiful young lady, we would have had no trouble. In reality, she wasn't that old, but to my young eyes she was. After walking quite a way in the hot sun, we finally did get a ride.

Once, two GIs who my folks knew and had had over to our house invited me to go to a private house that was being run as a club. They had drinks and went swimming in a large pool, while I just went swimming. To be able to swim in a pool with clean water was a great treat for me because I hadn't done it for three years. My folks really trusted the GIs to take care of me and they all did. None ever abused that trust.

An officer once took me to an afternoon at an officers' club and I got quickly bored watching him drink and dance with some American Red Cross women. I had no interest in women at that time and couldn't wait to get back to my buddies. Occasionally, I would see a truck of American Army nurses go by and once two of them came to our house on a visit. One of them was very pretty, but I was completely tongue-tied. I remember her telling Mom that I seemed to be very shy, and I sure was.

One evening, a GI from a nearby camp invited me to go to the camp movie with him that was held in a Quonset hut instead of in an open field. Being indoors, we were very comfortable, but the movie was late in getting there from another camp. The movie, *Meet Me in St. Louis*, was great, but it was midnight before I got home. That was one time my folks got worried about what had happened to me. The GI brought me home and explained the situation.

We still had GIs at our house to chat with in the evenings. We were always glad to have them come over because they were interesting to talk to about the States and they always brought some candy, cigarettes, or food along. In return, they certainly enjoyed our company and being in a nice house.

One evening in August, a bunch of them were at our house and we were all chatting when somehow the news came out that the Japanese had surrendered. They all cheered and went back to their camps to celebrate. After that, the camps were disassembled.

How Dad earned money at that time for us to live on I have no idea. A lot of what I remember is what I recall directly or what Mom told me when I asked her about the Japanese Occupation. I never asked her about the time immediately afterward. My folks' philosophy was that I shouldn't have to worry about such things and I didn't. Nor did I ask any questions about such matters. After all, the interesting thing for me was the war. As a matter of fact, I didn't think we had had anything that exciting happen to us because we hadn't been interned.

Many of those who had been interned told me later that they felt it was much more dangerous on the outside. Some women, whose husbands were away, found that they could not continue paying for living on the outside and asked to be interned. These were women of the Allied nations who because of illness, sick children, or other reasons did not have to go into camp originally, or in some cases were let out of camp. They found out that outside there was no support group and you were completely on your own. Inside the camp, overcrowded and restricted as it was, you did have your friends and you got food, housing and medicine at no cost, minimal as they may have been. When Manila was liberated, it was the first place the Army freed. Some families who could have gone into the camp, but opted not to go, were later raped and killed in the battle for Manila.

When I think back on it, it is ironic that throughout the bombing, shelling and fighting the only dead people I saw were after the Liberation, the dead Japanese soldier at the Peters' house, and the Filipino who had electrocuted himself. The closest I came to death during that time was the near turning over of the command car.

While the goat herd ate up more money in food than it brought in, and while it did not multiply and grow from new births or give us plenty of meat and more milk, it did save our lives. It did that by making us move out of Pax Court on Balagtas Street. Had we stayed there we would most likely have been killed. The court and the apartments across the street where the Japanese had kept their horses were razed to the ground.

While we were living in Pax Court, we met Dr. Walter Frankel, who lived in the house next to ours. He was also a German refugee like ourselves and a noted surgeon. From what I was told, during the fighting, the Japanese knocked on his door, and told him and his wife and sister to come with them. Though they protested that they were Germans and allies of the Japanese, it didn't matter. The Japanese took them and about a dozen Filipinos across the street into the apartments there, tied their hands,

piled up furniture around them, and then set fire to it. Anyone who moved was shot. Finally, a Filipino woman was able to untie them and the survivors fled, the Japanese having left by that time. Only Dr. Frankel, his sister, and two others survived.

Atrocities like this and worse were repeated throughout Manila south of the Pasig River, and that part of the city was thoroughly destroyed, while anyone such as ourselves in the northern part of the city came through relatively unscathed. I recently found out from Robert Hinds that he visited our Maytubig compound shortly after his liberation from Santo Tomas and all the houses in the compound had been destroyed. So, we were twice lucky—once moving out of Maytubig and then out of Pax Court.

The battle for Manila resulted in about 100,000 civilians killed and estimates are that sixty percent were due to Japanese atrocities and forty percent due to American shelling. As Mr. Lienhard told me recently, "We were very, very lucky".

Speaking of goats, I only recently realized that having been born on January 15, I am a Capricorn and therefore it is appropriate that the GOATS SAVED OUR LIVES AND POSSESSIONS. In astrology, Capricorn is the sign of the goat.

RODERICK HALL'S NARRATIVE

In Santo Tomas we had lots of great Army chow, and I was reunited with many friends I had not seen for three years. We hung around in several groups. There was not much to do, except to talk to GIs from time to time. For amusement, we played with firecrackers made by using the gunpowder

Photograph taken in Santo Tomas Internment Camp of Alastair Cameron Hall and his children, from left, Ian, Consuelo, Alastair, Roderick: March 1945.
Photograph taken by unknown G.I.

tation home in the USA, and other Allied countries. Since our house was intact, at the end of March we left Santo Tomas and all moved back together with Uncle Joe and Aunt Mercedes. Her family had moved to Calatagan in Batangas Province in October 1944. They had asked us to join them, but a family conference believed we would be safer in Manila, so we had remained, a decision that cost my family their lives.

There were still no utilities, but we were able to get a generator and a water trailer that was filled regularly from the Army. Shortly after our return, I found Dad digging in the ground near the front steps, as if searching. He was looking for a glass jar that held all the family's jewelry, which had been buried at the beginning of the war. I told him I'd seen Uncle Alfred dig up a jar a few weeks before the battles had begun. I didn't know where he had put it, but grandmother had a safe in the house that was painted to look like a piece of furniture. On returning to the house, we had found it in the garden, blown open and empty.

We discovered that our family silver, looted from the home, was for sale in the local open air markets. Two MPs accompanied Ian and me to the markets, and as we pointed out our silver, the MPs took them, and returned them to us. Several "recovery" trips were made to the San Andres and Paco markets.

Uncle Joe was still on General MacArthur's staff, so we had Generals and Colonels for lunch and dinner every day. Ian and I would sometimes bring a friend for lunch, generally a private or corporal camped nearby. They were usually awed by all the brass. One day a USO show came to town, and the star, comedian Joe E. Brown came to lunch before the show. I rode with him to the show, and he kept leaning out of the car, flashing his well-known big smile.

taken from bullets. They exploded with a loud noise and could cause burns if held in the hand. We developed a kind of Russian roulette game. Standing in a circle, one boy would light a fire cracker, and we would quickly toss this among us. There were no serious injuries, but a few burns.

Most evenings at dusk, we sat outside the gymnasium building with Dad and Father Daly, an American Missionary who had spent many years in China. They both smoked hand-rolled cigarettes, using fine paper pages torn from a prayer book. Father Daly later returned to his missionary work in China.

A few at a time, our friends disappeared, as the Red Cross arranged their transpor-

A unit of the 37th Infantry Division camped under tents in the grounds of the Assumption Convent, half a block from the house, pulled back from fighting for two weeks of rest, before returning to the front lines. Not having any school, and with not much to do, we usually visited the soldiers every day. Living with guns and fighting, the soldiers played around with explosives. One of their tricks was to unscrew the top of a hand grenade, empty out the powder and remove the percussion cap. This made the grenade a dud. I can remember going home for lunch with a dud grenade, pulled the pin and threw it on the sofa. The Colonels sitting on it quickly dove over the sides! I thought it was funny, but caught hell!

WAC Captain Juanita Sudduth Stryker

I made good friends with a Browning Automatic Rifle (BAR) man, Pentti Metzapalto, about 20 years old. He was from Minnesota, and his parents were immigrants from Finland. He wanted extra bandoliers to carry ammunition, so we went to the ruined Legislature Building to explore. A GI with us found some US$20 gold pieces, and Pentti found some discarded US Army bandoliers. Unfortunately, Pentti was killed by friendly fire shortly after his return to the front.

From time to time there would be awful smells at home and Ian and I would enter the ruins surrounding the house and track down the source. Invariably it was a corpse, so we would call the Army who would remove the body. Years later, in 1949, Ian and his classmate, Leo Schwaiger, were assigned a biology project for school. I pointed out where we had buried a Japanese soldier. Ian and Leo dug out the skeleton and assembled it for the class project. The toes were easily assembled as they had stayed neatly in place inside the split-toed shoes.

Ian and I remained in Manila until May 24, 1945. Dad worried that we were losing too much school and decided we should go to Edinburgh, Scotland, to live with our paternal grandmother and attend school. Dad made arrangements with the Red Cross, and the afternoon before we left we spent the night in Santo Tomas, to be ready to leave very early in the morning. There he introduced us to Bill McLaren, a Scottish bachelor of about 35 years of age, who was returning to Glasgow, Scotland. Bill agreed to chaperone us on the trip. In the morning the entire departing group went down to the beach area and boarded a landing craft that had its ramp down. It ferried us to our transport ship. Ian and I were young enough to have a berth in the officers' quarters with families, but since Bill McLaren could not join us, we chose to stay with him, down in the holds where the bunks were stacked four high, and full of GIs returning to the States. In spite of this, we had the run of the ship, and only saw Bill about 3 times during the three week trip.

First stop was Leyte, where the ship took on about 500 wounded soldiers, many in body casts. The first day at sea most of us young boys had our hair shaved off, and petroleum jelly put on, in case we had lice.

From Leyte, because of submarine danger, we zigzagged our way across the Pacific. Our tranquil days were interrupted when we were diverted to Honolulu. We sailed into Honolulu Bay, a Navy tender came out to meet us and delivered its important cargo, 2 Senators and 3 Congressmen. Our ship then turned and sailed away. We probably did not get closer than ten miles from Waikiki. Finally sailing under the Golden Gate, we moored at Fort Mason. The Red Cross arranged rooms for us in the only place available, a fleabag hotel on Third Street, South of Market Street, a rough area.

We spent about 10 days in San Francisco until seats were found on the long train ride to Chicago, where we transferred stations and continued to New York. I don't remember much about New York, except that one day we went to Coney Island, and a man offered to pay us a prize if he could not guess where we were from by our accent. Naturally he lost. I can't imagine how he could have come up with Manila!

Passage was finally found for us on an old banana boat sailing to Liverpool. It had five large crates lashed to the deck of this rusted small boat. They contained small planes with wings removed. The trip was estimated to take five days, but the engine broke down and we floated in the Sargasso Sea while the engine was repaired. This was great fun, because as we floated in a sea covered with seaweed almost to the horizon, we spent our days trying to catch some of the many little crabs that lived in the seaweed. Being a small boat, the sea was only about 10 feet below the railing. The crossing took ten days, and Ian and I finally arrived in Liverpool where our two aunts met us and took us the next day by train to Edinburgh. Since hotel rooms were not available, we spent the night with friends of the family, also called Hall. As I was the eldest male guest, Mr Hall asked me to say grace. I was ashamed to tell him that I did not know how to do it!

In Manila, Ian and I had watched the fireworks celebrating Germany's surrender. On August 15th we joined the large crowds on Princes Street in Edinburgh to celebrate Japan's surrender. The following summer Dad wrote to say he was to remarry. At that point I broke down and cried for the first time over my mother's death. I had clung to the hope that Mom had escaped and was hiding in the mountains, but would return one day. Dad's letter made me realize this would not happen. In August 1946 Dad and his new bride Juanita Sudduth spent one month with us in Edinburgh on their honeymoon. This was the start of a long and happy relationship. Dad died in 1971, but Juanita was a wonderful and loving stepmother to the four of us for sixty one years, passing away quietly in December 2007, aged 101.

Roderick and Ian Hall, San Francisco, June 1945

Ian and I spent three happy years living with our grandmother and attending school in Edinburgh. We wrote weekly to Dad. In 1948, as things settled, Dad asked if we wanted to return and finish school in Manila. Both jumped at the chance. At the end of Summer term in Edinburgh, we took the train to London, spending five days sightseeing and at the 1948 London Olympics. Our Pan American flight was delayed two days in Rome by fog in Istanbul, then went through Damascus to Karachi and Calcutta. Seeing two boys travelling alone, and with the city convulsed by religious riots, the stewardesses suggested we stay at the crew house, a large colonial mansion run by a widowed English lady. In those days Pan Am flew East from New York, and West from San Francisco, both terminating in Calcutta. Our flight from San Francisco had not arrived, so we waited, unable to leave the house as groups of marauding men roamed the streets looking for people to assault. The next day we flew on to Manila via Bangkok. Since the Manila school term had already started, we started school almost immediately. Two years later I was a member of the High School graduating Class of 1950 at the American School. Several classmates had started with me in kindergarten. We had lived through the war, and were now finishing school together.

For many years, well into my twenties, I had a recurring dream. I hid in the thick vegetation of the Assumption Convent garden while Japanese soldiers searched for me, walking within inches of where I lay. I would suddenly wake up.

Sitting on the garden bench in Manila in 1948.
First Row (left to right): Alaistair "Allie" Hall; our father, Alaistair "Shorty" Hall; Juanita S. Hall (our step-mother and our father's second wife).
Second Row (left to right): Ian Hall; Roderick Hall.

An old Chinese proverb says "May you live in interesting times." Nine short years after experiencing the battle for Manila, having graduated from university in California, and now a light weapons infantry GI myself, I shipped out from Seattle, Washington, on another military transport, bound for Korea, and an eighteen -month tour of duty. Again I crossed the International Date Line by ship, this time missing my birthday as we lost a day.

HANS HOEFLEIN'S NARRATIVE

In our friend's house, we rented a large room and a kitchen and we shared a bathroom. We stayed there until March or April of 1946.

Shortly after we were liberated, my father went down to what he thought would

Hans Hoeflein in Manila in 1945 (age 14).

be the ruins of Philippine Engineering Corporation. To his surprise the building was intact and there were 300 Filipinos saying, "Mr. Hoeflein, tell us what to do." Mr. Sampson, the previous owner, went back to the States and let my dad continue to run the company. The Japanese had left some rice and an old truck there and so two or three days after being liberated, Philippine Engineering was back in business. As for me, Mrs. Walser, another friend of our family tutored me and some other kids until the American School reopened in late 1946.

In the fall of 1945 there were some picket boats moored on the Pasig River near where we lived on Nagtahan Street. Through meeting some of the officers attached to the War Crimes Investigation Unit that lived on these boats, I was able to go around to some of the Southern Islands on a small Army cargo ship. This ship went to some of the more out-of-the-way islands to interview witnesses for the Japanese War Crime Trials in Manila and Tokyo. All in all, it was a very interesting experience.

HANS WALSER'S NARRATIVE

Although my mother was an American with an American passport, my father and I were Swiss with Swiss passports. After a lot of negotiations, my father got all three of us passage on an American troop ship going back to the United States. My mother's sister in Iowa was willing to sponsor us so that we could get into the States. We sailed on the USS Eberly. A truck took us from Santo Tomas to the pier and we had a long barge ride out to the ship. This was April 9th. My first meal on the ship was great. However, I threw up. Again, the food was too rich for my stomach. The ship was the standard troop ship with a lot of bunks on top of one another to the ceiling. It was jammed full. We ran into a storm that was very bad with waves sweeping way over the decks. All the passengers were put down into their cabins with the doors shut. The air got very stale. With the ship tossing side to side, some of the things people had with them that were on the floor, started rolling from one side to the other. With the motion of the ship and the stale air, one passenger got sick and threw up. Since the doors were shut, the smell made another person sick and he threw up. Soon everyone was sick and throwing up. The stench was terrible. But after a few hours, we got out of the storm, the doors were open and we could go out on deck and breathe fresh air.

We had been sailing only for a few days when we came upon a sight I will never forget. We arrived at Bikini Atoll and specifically Eniwetok (where they later dropped an atomic bomb for testing). Around us were hundreds and hundreds of ships, from aircraft carriers to PT boats. I think this was the massing of ships for the landing of Iwo Jima or for Japan itself. It was an unbelievable sight.

From there we sailed on to the United States, arriving at San Pedro by Los Angeles. I entered the United States as a cross-dresser. By now my polo shirt and shorts were a mess since those were the only clothes I had. It was decided that I couldn't go ashore looking tattered and dirty. But I was only 12 years old and pretty short. No GI clothes would fit me. So I was outfitted with a WAC (Women's Army Corps) blouse, shorts, shoes and socks. From there we took a train to Ames, Iowa, where my aunt, uncle and 3 cousins lived. We stayed several days with them and then got an apartment across the street. My father went to New York City where he worked for that branch of Zuellig, the company he worked for during the war. He stayed there for a year and then went back

to Manila. My mother taught mathematics at Iowa State College and I went to school in Ames. We stayed there 3 years and then joined my father in Manila. We lived in a reconstructed apartment on Balagtas Street, the same complex I mentioned during the war that the Japanese soldiers had occupied during the liberation. I went to the American School and graduated high school from that school as did the other 3 writers of this book

Curiously, I do not have a single photograph taken by anyone in my family during the entire 3¼ year occupation. Either we never took any or they got destroyed in the fire.

It took me years before I could eat rice again. I had eaten it three times a day in various forms for so long. I still don't care for coconut. I still don't laugh out loud. I

Aerial view of the Walled City of Manila in May 1945

still find it very hard to be confrontational when I should. For years I could not be in the company of a Japanese. Early on in my business career in the early 60s, I even had to check out of a hotel in Washington, D.C. that I had just checked into, when I saw a crowd of Japanese businessmen in the lobby. A few times in my working career, when times got really rough, I would tell myself that I had survived a "massacre" and since I had survived that, I could easily survive this. And I did.

Looking back on those days, brings me a lot of admiration for my parents. While I didn't really have a full appreciation of what was happening, my parents certainly did. Several decisions had to be made every single day. And these were life and death decisions. The decision of which yard to be in each day was crucial. Later in life, I wrestled with the obvious question of why we survived when most of the people around us did not. I have come to peace with that question. But it is still hard, 63 years later, to like the Japanese.